MIRÓ

The Life of a Passion

LLUÍS PERMANYER

MIRÓ

The Life of a Passion

English translation by Paul Martin

Edicions de 1984
Barcelona

Miró
La vida d'una passió
© Lluís Permanyer, 2003

First edition: April 2003
Second edition: August 2014
Design: Enric Satué
Photographic rights: Català-Roca,
Ferran Freixa i Joaquim Gomis
For the illustrations by Joan Miró, © Successió Miró, 2014
English translation: Paul Martin
© for this edition: Edicions de 1984, S.L.
Trafalgar, 10, 2n, 08010 Barcelona
e-mail:1984@edicions1984.cat
www.edicions1984.cat

Printed by Novagràfik

ISBN: 84-96061-09-4
Legal deposit: B.15975-2003

INDEX

INDEX

PROLOGUE

His painting attracted me the moment I discovered it. With my first wages I bought a lithograph by him. I was introduced to him by Joan Gaspar in 1963. After a while I began to meet him regularly, and soon there developed a natural trust between us, to the point that he began to confide certain things to me. In these circumstances, it was quite easy for me one day to suggest that I write his memoirs for him. Not only did he agree enthusiastically, but a few weeks later he showed me his diary, with annotations on a few pages, and told me, "I'm writing down some recollections ready to begin working with you." But shortly afterwards he told me, "I'm sorry, but I've realised I'll have to give up on my memoirs. I'd have to talk about things that are too personal, about my parents, my wife and my daughter. And I think perhaps I don't have any right to do that." I tried to persuade him with various arguments – that the memoirs would not be published until years, decades even, after his death; that he could relate the more delicate situations with discretion, because the same thing can be told in several ways; or that he could even make no mention at all of certain episodes. And he answered me, "Look, when I accepted your proposal, I did it because I wanted to go to the bottom of things, to the point that I was thinking of telling you about my life as if I were lying on the psychiatrist's couch. That's to say, I wanted, I needed, to tell it all, absolutely everything. And when I take a decision, I always intend to throw myself into it head-first; I've got no time for halfway measures." And with that he gave me a dry-point engraving, a very powerful one that I had seen him create by scoring the copper plate with an iron nail, all the while telling me of the sensations he felt and what he intended with each line. That engraving, that became so special to me, has this printed dedication: "To Lluís Permanyer, in memory of a few days of working together. 27-IX-79."

In this biography I speak only of the human facet of Joan Miró, as the publisher asked me to. It is not a work of research: the aim was to write a book to be read, not another contribution to a mass of details or discoveries. And this commission has been very interesting, because I have to admit that until now I had always pushed this facet aside, concentrating solely on his work in everything I wrote about him. It has been a great pleasure for me to pursue this evocation, because I have recovered a considerable amount of information and experiences that at the time I did not use or even undervalued. I must emphasise the extraordinary, moving human quality of the man. He never sought it, but everyone who knew him respected him and expressed sincere affection for him, something none too common in so many figures so arrogantly enthroned on the heights of Olympus. I was very fond of him and I still miss him, much more often than either of us could even have suspected back then.

THEY WANTED A GIRL

Joan Miró i Ferrà was born on 20 April, 1893, at nine o'clock in the evening, in a bedroom to the left of the first-floor dining room of his family's house at number 4 of Passatge del Crèdit in Barcelona. On one occasion he remarked that "I once read that my birthday coincides with Mao Tse Tung's," and confessed that if this was true he was delighted. He was mistaken: the Chinese revolutionary was born on 26 December of the same year. Miró's father, Miquel Miró i Adzerias, the son of a blacksmith from Cornudella (Tarragona), after doing his apprenticeship in Reus, decided to go and live in Barcelona. It is not true that he was a jeweller, as all of Miró's biographers say. "My father was a backroom watchmaker," the artist himself told me one day when he was revealing to me certain confidences about his unhappy youth, wanting to bring his father's professional category down to its true level. And the workshop was a tiny room in the entrance way of the house at Carrer Ferran 34. But the business gradually expanded, to the point that his father opened the jewellery shop El Acuárium at number 4 of the Plaça Reial. Miró's father was not, then, a goldsmith, a profession the artist only related with Ramon Sunyer, his friend from the School of Fine Arts whose portrait he painted.

The boy was given the forename of his maternal grandfather, Joan Ferrà, the son of a Palma shoe shop owner, who specialised in making cane rocking chairs and eventually gained prestige as a cabinet-maker, even creating a number of pieces of furniture which were commissioned from him by Queen Isabel II of Spain during a visit to Mallorca. He and his wife had both been born in Barcelona, but they moved to Palma and bought the house at Carrer Minyones 11. He was quite a character: he was illiterate and could only speak the Mallorcan dialect of Catalan, but he had earned himself a very comfortable position in life. He had a certain charm and the gift of conversation: he had travelled a lot, always by express train, even to Russia, and his grandson confessed to having great affection for him, having been lucky enough to spend a lot of time with him during his summers in the island, where he was sent on the mail boat under the care of the ship's purser.

The moment Joan was born, he was met with a scornful "I wanted a girl!" and was left naked and trembling on the cold marble. This was how he described to me, with saddened eyes and tight lips, his arrival in this world. And unfortunately this was a premonition. This family atmosphere has been very well portrayed in Rosa Maria Malet's biography of the artist.

At the age of seven, in 1900, he was sent to a private school at Carrer Regomir 13. He quickly turned out to be a poor student, perhaps because he discovered an even more suffocating atmosphere there than at home. He liked geography, but in sciences he was a disaster. His discomfort did nothing for his charac-ter, and he became absent-minded, solitary, taciturn.

Joan Miró with his parents and sister.

The only ray of sunlight in his school day was the drawing class given by Mr. Civil, which allowed him to escape from an almost unbearable routine, to find relief from a disheartening atmosphere. He always washed his hands very carefully before even touching his paper or pencils; his working instruments were already like sacred objects to him, and this ritual no doubt aided his concentration. This was the beginning of a very characteristic trait in him, a faithful arrangement of his working ambience: it reminds me of the Japanese tea ceremony or the mental preparation of oriental calligraphers before setting pen to paper.

Curiously enough, Miró could never manage to paint a face copied from an engraving, but he would lovingly, and accurately, paint the leaves of a tree one by one. For this reason he started drawing landscapes, particularly during his stays at his respective grandparents" homes in Cornudella and Palma. And he began to neglect his studies. In his later years, seeing a photograph of himself dressed up for his first communion, he recognised that what he saw was a boy who did drawings rather than a student of the catechism. And this memory did not bring him the slightest pleasure: at nights he was tortured by fear, terrified of having forgotten some sin during confession. He was already revealing a mixture of ethical principles and a scrupulous, responsible nature.

His school reports confirmed over and over again that as a student he was going from bad to worse, which plunged his parents into despair. He could barely write when he scrawled this solemn declaration on a Christmas card: "I inform you that I want to be a painter." In spite of that, and with the confirmation of his incapacity for study, in 1907 his father decided to enrol him in a commercial school, with the idea that he would complete his apprenticeship with his maternal uncle, who had a merchant's business in London. A way had to be found for the boy to make his living, since he seemed to have no interest in anything except drawing. And he was so dogged in this, without reaching the point of rebellion, that his father finally agreed to let him combine his commerce course with evening classes at the School of Fine Arts. The result was another resounding failure: he was disgusted by everything that smacked of commerce, and his art teachers were alarmingly mediocre. The only benefit he reaped was to come under the influence of the painters Modest Urgell and Josep Pascó and to make friends with another student who he would grow to love like a brother: Joan Prats.

Of Modest Urgell, Miró conserved something more than good memories: he was greatly influenced by Urgell's unmistakeable way of structuring his enormous paintings with their large empty spaces, separated across the middle by a powerful, entrancing horizon. Miró acknowledged that for three forms which became an obsession in his work – a red circle, the moon and a star – he was indebted to Urgell. Josep Pascó was far from being a great painter, but he instilled in the young Miró a love for art and a cultivation of patience with technique; it is no coincidence that his best works were the decoration of the apartment of his famous artist friend Ramon Casas (at Passeig de Gràcia 96) and the "goldfish bowl" and "round hall" of the Cercle del Liceu. Moreover, Pascó was the type of teacher who encouraged his students: one day, in front of all of the class, he praised the violent colours Miró had boldly painted on his canvas, and in doing so he became perhaps the first person to discover Miró's innate sensibility for colour. The youngster was also thrilled that Pascó urged him to buy his first palette and set of paints, and encouraged him not to be afraid to express himself with total freedom instead of suffocating inside the straitjacket of academic art. It is no surprise that Miró decided to continue taking classes from Pascó.

When Miró finished his commercial studies in 1910, his father obliged him to enter the accountancy profession, as an unpaid trainee at the Dalmau Oliveres medical warehouse at number 14 of Passeig de la Indústria (now Passeig de Picasso). He was told that the company closed every evening at 7.30, which meant he could still hope to continue his classes at the nearby School of Fine Arts, which ran from 7.00

to 9.00, even if he arrived late. But in reality things did not work out that way. He started work every morning at 8.00, and in order to sleep as long as possible he calculated that he could walk to work in seven minutes. On arriving, he had to write his name in chalk on a small slate, and lateness was penalised. The lunch break was from 1.00 to 3.00, and in the afternoon work invariably went on long beyond the supposed closing time of 7.30; in fact he rarely escaped from the yoke before 9.00. On Saturdays, too, he worked all day, but finished a little earlier. As if that were not enough, he had to report for work on Sundays too, from 9.00 to 2.00, to put the papers in order. Holidays were, naturally, out of the question. Miró summed up the experience as "Three years of slavery: they treated us despicably, like animals." To make matters worse, on Saturdays, when he finished earlier, he had to take the train to Montgat and then a coach to Teià, where his parents had rented a small house. The routine was exhausting, and aggravated by being totally imposed on him. And to cap it all, his father wanted him to study English so that he could go and work for his uncle in London.

It is no surprise, then, that eventually Miró not only gave up his classes at the School of Fine Arts but even lost all interest in picking up a pencil and drawing. On the other hand, at work he found it impossible to concentrate, and without realising it he often drew doodles in his accounts books, which naturally won him a severe reprimand. On arriving home he did not find peace and quiet but quite the opposite: arguments with his father due to his stubborn insistence on wanting to be a painter. His father assured him that art was not a profession for earning a living,

14

Joan Miró dressed for his First Communion.

that what the boy had to do was find a position in life: a perfectly bourgeois idea of life and the future. He even insinuated that if Joan did not give up the idea of painting, he would force him to go into the church or the army. Sometimes the two went shooting together: their walks eased their relationship somewhat, but when Joan commented, for instance, that he saw a violet-coloured sky, his father would laugh at him and call him a lunatic, infuriating the boy with such a flagrant lack of sympathy and understanding.

After almost two years of this inhuman routine, Miró's physical fatigue was suddenly aggravated by mental exhaustion, plunging him into a depression that left his body defenceless and easy prey to a typhoid fever. He spent two months in bed, subjected to a strict, irrational diet that almost brought him to the door of death. But it was not yet his time, and almost miraculously he survived.

To favour a rapid recovery, his parents decided to move him to a healthier place than a Barcelona apartment. They sent him to the Mas d'en Ferratges, a farmhouse surrounded by vineyards and olive groves that they had bought a couple of years earlier outside the village of Mont-roig, in Tarragona, to spend their summers. And it was no ordinary property. Josep Maria Martí Rom has established that it previously belonged to Antoni Ferratges i de Mesa, the Marquis of Mont-roig, a liberal senator in the Madrid Parliament and the first editor of the recently-founded Barcelona newspaper *La Vanguardia*.

It was here in Mont-roig that Joan Miró began to dedicate himself to painting. His father had finally accepted that this was an irrevocable vocation, and had given in to the dramatic way his son had expressed his determination. Miró made a fast and thorough recovery. From then on, Mont-roig represented an almost mythical place for him, to which he had to return periodically to recharge his batteries with its particular and irreplaceable energy.

"My mother," Miró said, "was very intelligent, very open-minded, a woman of great personality. The opposite of my father, who did not treat me well at all. She always loved me very much, and she used to cry when she saw I was going in the wrong direction. Later on she took a lively interest in my work. My sister [Dolors, who was born four years after Joan, and whose arrival presumably eased their mother's earlier disappointment at Joan's birth and enabled her to love the two equally] was very fond of me, even tough she had a very different character. She was a generous soul: when I was broke and couldn't buy paints, she used to give me money in secret."

In 1912, Miró was permitted to enrol at the Galí art school in Barcelona, where he went from 3.00 to 5.00 in the afternoons before going on to the Cercle de Sant Lluc from 7.00 to 9.00. Francesc d'Assís Galí was a painter who had decided to open a school on the top floor of the building at number 4, Carrer de Cucurulla. His teaching method was advanced, unconventional and Italian-influenced, and he strove to promote all facets of his students cultural life, organising concerts, outings to the countryside and commented readings, mainly of poets. The school's credo was clearly rooted in 19th-century principles of controlling emotional impulse and romantic whim. Galí also showed his students books and magazines which reproduced the works of modern painters like the Impressionists and the *Fauves*. When they went on an outing, Miró said, "we carried no brushes or paints, we only went to look: Galí told us to wear a crown of eyes on our heads." That experience, along with the discovery in Romanesque murals of angels whose wings were covered with eyes, caused an enormous impression on Miró which he was soon to express, and he went on to use this symbolic resource very extensively.

Another great breakthrough for Miró was learning to "see" with his fingers and hands. He had demonstrated over and over again that he was entirely incapable of drawing the profiles of people and objects. He could not even distinguish a straight line from a curve. Once Galí realised that Miró was a born colourist who was unable to perceive form, he made him touch and feel objects with his eyes closed and then draw them as he had perceived them with his hands. In this way Miró revealed an unusual sensitivity for volume, which would lead him decades later to explore the techniques of sculpture. It was clear that Miró was not endowed with artistic gifts, but had boundless self-denial and willpower. He learned to work hard and apply himself to overcome a marked lack of ability: what was a defect became, in time, a virtue that prevented him from falling into that mannerism that has ruined so many creators who have been let themselves be carried away by the gifts they have displayed since their early days. It is no surprise, then, that he was wary of Picasso's preciosity and that in 1915 he wrote to the poet Bartomeu Ferrà that "man needs struggle, as Goethe said in *Tridon and Amida.*" Not surprisingly, one day Miró's father walked into the school and asked Galí if it was true that the students had spent the whole day walking in

18

the Montseny hills; his son had arrived home without even a hasty sketch in his notebook, and had told his father that he had been whistling Beethoven's *Pastorale* all day. When Galí confirmed that it was all true, Miró's father sternly replied that he wanted his son to be a painter, not a musician!

Miró discovered Cubism through the exhibitions organised by Josep Dalmau, an art and antiques dealer who was martyred by the avant-garde, whose gallery was hidden away at the end of a narrow passage at number 18 of Carrer de la Portaferrissa. Miró used to visit these exhibitions with fellow students like Josep F. Ràfols, Enric Cristòfol Ricart and his old friend Joan Prats. With Prats he also used to walk up into the hills of Horta and Tibidabo on painting excursions. Prats was the son of the owner of a wellknown hat shop in Carrer Ferran, and when he realised he had little future as a painter he entered the family business. Miró said that he had made "a kind of blood transfusion" with Prats, and that "until he died he was my closest friend, a brother." Prats gradually built up a fabulous collection of Miró's works, which at first were gifts and were later 'exchanged' for hats: the young Miró was quite a dandy, and the right hat was an essential part of his clothing, which became more and more impeccable. I remember that the window of the Prats shop, transferred to Rambla de Catalunya, had only two or three hats, a mobile by Alexander Calder and a collage by Miró proclaiming *Prats is quality*. Miró would discuss any doubt with Prats, and his friend's last piece of advice to him before dying in 1970 was to urge him to set up a foundation in his native city.

Before dinner every evening, Miró would spend a

couple of hours at the Cercle Artístic de Sant Lluc, a school created by the Llimona brothers, avid church-goers who had left the Cercle Artístic for grotesque reasons of extreme puritanism. The school was located in what had formerly been the legendary artists' bar Els Quatre Gats, frequented by established figures like Rusiñol and Casas and emerging painters like Picasso and Nonell. Here Miró came into contact with a figure who was to influence his work: no less than the young Antoni Gaudí, another student of the school. Miró realised that Gaudí had little natural talent for drawing a model from life but made up for this lack with great dedication: a lesson in humility and application. "During the quarter-hour break we got into conversations where it seemed the world would catch fire. The concierge sold paints and often let us pay him later. And he prepared snacks for us, bread and tomato. We were very happy there."

I suspect that this kind of atmosphere helped to offset his withdrawn nature, his inclination to solitude and silence, to hardly ever talk about his feelings. The cheerful air of the school neutralised Miró's innate pessimism and tragic view of life, a characteristic he freely acknowledged on several occasions. It was then that, having overcome his family's hostility, he also began to paint at home, in a small room on the second floor. Although he continued to attend classes at the Sant Lluc school for years, at least until 1918, his good friend Sebastià Gasch, the author of one of the first articles defending him, never forgot his lack of ability: "when he was drawing, he gave the impression of suffering horribly: he used to stick his tongue out like a child struggling to write the first letters of the alphabet."

The beneficial effect of this relationship with other budding artists is confirmed by the fact that in 1914 he rented his first studio, sharing it with Ricart. It was in an alley called Carrer de l'Arc de Figueres, which disappeared when the Via Laietana was opened up. The two young painters stayed there until 1916, when they moved to number 51 of Carrer de Sant Pere Més Baix, where they paid 15 pesetas. In 1918 Ricart moved to Paris, a decision which would later influence Miró. For the time being, however, he stayed in the studio alone, delighted to discover that the house opposite was the birthplace of Isidre Nonell (who died in 1911) and that the family still ran a pasta shop there. It is possible that Miró thought of Nonell and his colleague Ricart, precisely when he was incapable of transferring any idea to cánvas, tortured by a disorientation and despair that even led him to bang his head against the wall.

From December 1914 until February 1915, Miró lived with his mother in Caldetes, where he had gone to recover from a bout of typhoid. I think this period of living alone together brought them closer.

In 1915, the always smartly-dressed Miró was dismayed to find himself forced to put on uniform, on being called up to do his military service. He was stationed in Barcelona itself, and perhaps in order not to be recognised by acquaintances he grew a moustache: in Ricart's oil portrait of him, he has an almost military air. Miró told Melià some details about this period: "I was in the Bergara Infantry Regiment number 57. I was just a private, of course. I think I was a good soldier: I used to salute energetically and I was a good shot. As this was during the First World War and it wasn't clear what was likely to happen, the training was very hard. We had to guard the prison: everyone felt the cold, and although it was forbidden to talk to the prisoners we used to swap things with them. I've got a still life with a goldfinch [*North-South*, 1917], and in it there's a purse woven in lots of different-coloured wools, made by one of the prisoners." Miró's family had paid a 'quota' to make his military service easier: it lasted until 1917, but he only had to spend three months each year in the barracks. The guard duties were, of course, long and tedious, and in the light of the lamps Miró took to doing something forbidden: reading. He discovered Apollinaire in the pages of *Le poète assassiné*, and he began to take a lively interest in literature of this type and quality.

There is no doubt that military service made it impossible for Miró to concentrate fully on his painting, but he did manage to produce a series of portraits from life in the Fauvist style. The models were his friends, who were always patient, and whose profiles he knew better than anyone. One night in a café, Ricart commented that in Miró's portrait of him, his hand had six fingers; Miró, incredulous, insisted on seeing it for himself and hurried to correct it by candle light (at two o'clock in the morning.

He also painted a portrait of Juanita Obrador, the daughter of the owner of the boarding house where Ricart lived. Both Juanita and Ricart were from Vilanova, and there was a certain confidence between them, so one day, after observing in horror how her portrait was evolving during the endless sittings, Juanita could not resist the temptation to ask Ricart if his painter friend was not perhaps a dangerous lunatic. One day Miró broke a glass pane in the stair-

Joan Miró with Lluís Permanyer, the author.

way, and having no money to replace it, he was told to leave the house and never come back. He had to finish the portrait from memory.

He never seemed to have a penny, yet he was always smartly dressed. A photograph from this period shows him wearing a stiff collar, a bow tie, a waistcoat crossed by a watch chain, and an immaculately-fitting suit of good-quality cloth. I wonder if Miró was already having his shirts made by Queralt the tailor, whose workshop in Reus he used to visit until his old age, often accompanied by Paco Farreras, the director of the Maeght Gallery. Ricart used to say that even when they went to the studio to paint on Sundays, Miró would always turn up in his finest clothes, with pale yellow gloves, beige spats and a walking stick. And in this guise he was glad to go slumming in the

Joan Miró as a young man.

notorious 'Chinese Quarter' with Gasch and Prats. They admitted to being fascinated by the neighbourhood's dissolute fauna, fetid smells and sordid scenes, and they enjoyed singing the praises of the graffiti that livened up its cracked and crumbling walls. But what really captured their attention was the display window of the chemist's shop in the infamous Carrer de l'Arc del Teatre, dominated by the startling presence of incredible, huge, even brutal sexual aids. Miró told me that they saw these terrifying monsters, made of thick rubber with triangular knobs attached, as genuine sculptures, forms with resonances of black art which foreshadowed what would soon be created in Paris under the umbrella of Surrealism. Prats pointed out that although Miró was always one of the group on those excursions, he was invariably the first to go home, for he was never a client of the brothels. I suppose he preferred the Avinguda Paral·lel, Barcelona's theatrical thoroughfare of the time, where he was taken by the firm hand of Gasch, a lover of the *café-concerts* in all their infinite variety. There he began to develop a taste for flamenco music and dance, to which he remained faithful for the rest of his life; good proof of this is a delightful photograph taken by his friend Francesc Català Roca, taken in the 1960's, showing Miró absorbed in the magic of the dancer *La Chunga.*

In 1916 Miró met the art dealer and gallery owner Josep Dalmau, a vital event for him at this formative time of his life. Dalmau was also an antiques dealer, but he was to go down in history as the apostle, or rather the martyr, of early Surrealism, particularly in these parts. He welcomed Miró warmly, and the young artist was soon regularly attending the informal debates that Dalmau hosted at his gallery in the evenings. Apart from the eager young local artists, the group included a number of foreign creators – Gleizes, Raynal, the Delaunays, Charchoune, Grunhoff and others – who had taken refuge in Barcelona from the German army's brutal bombardment of Paris. One of Dalmau's many feats was to bring Van Dongen to the gallery. "I remember him very well," Miró said, "stepping out of the car with his canvases rolled up under his arm." In that contagious atmosphere, Picabia's work made a dazzling impact with its light-heartedness, its radical rupturism and its visual and literary creativity (exemplified in the review *291*). Miró never met Picabia, even though in his later years he told Raillard that he used to see Picabia every evening at the Dalmau Galleries; the fact is made clear by a letter sent by Picabia in 1925 to Miró, in Paris, saying "I will be delighted to meet you in person."

All of this demonstrates that Miró was ready to take on board everything Dada stood for, but as he said in his later years, "Dalmau had never talked to me about the Dadaists." And indeed it was not the same to merely see the work, like that of all of the modern French artists Vollard brought to the great Exhibition of French Art in mid-1917, including Duchamp's formidable *Nu descendant l'escalier* (the first time it was displayed outside France), as it was to get to know the creators and even become friends with them, as Miró was soon to do in Paris. Looking back in his old age, Miró confessed to Raillard that at that time his home town had nothing to interest him, with the exception of Gaudí and the Modernist style with its houses, shops, grilles, ceramics and sculptures, the 'Butterfly House' … all of those things that, he added, "the idiots have destroyed." His curiosity was not limited to art and literature; although he never had money, he did not fail to attend the Liceu to be carried away by avant-garde ballets like Satie's *Parade* (in 1917) or Stravinsky's *Petrushka* (in 1918).

In the solitude of Mont-roig he strove to absorb all of these stimuli and to reflect them on canvas. He explored specific parts of the Tarragona countryside, which by now had become magical to him, and with fruitful results. He talked about it in a letter to Ricart in 1917: "The solitary life in Siurana, the primitivism of those admirable people, this intense work of mine and, above all, my spiritual confinement (...) have

La Chunga, a possible inspiration for the artist.

shut me inside myself, and as I have grown more sceptical towards everything that surrounds me, I have grown closer to God, the Trees and the Mountains and to Friendship." He told me with a smile that during the winters only two people remained in the windswept clifftop village of Siurana – and they were such bitter enemies that they never exchanged a word!

FIRST INSULTS AND MOCKERIES

He was beginning to find his way as a painter, he had worked very hard, he was starting to be influenced by an Orientalism which led him to produce miniatures and to work in what he called calligraphy. Finally he showed these works to Dalmau, with the intention of exhibiting them. Dalmau encouraged him but made him wait for almost two years. The time seemed endless, but that year of 1918 was to be a milestone for Miró. On 16 February, at the Dalmau Galleries, he inaugurated his first individual exhibition, having previously only displayed a few drawings or paintings in unimportant collective showings. It was an important exhibition, including not only 64 paintings but also a number of drawings. But its impact was undeniably negative, immediately provoking reactions that in some cases bordered on violence. People were shocked; Miró was ridiculed; someone manipulated the acrostic Josep Maria Junoy had created as a presentation and made it insulting; and a long letter in the form of a manifesto was written, being inspired, or so the critic Rafael Santos Torroella suspects, by the potter Josep 'Papitu' Llorens Artigas. The exhibition remained open until 3 March, which even allowed time for the works to be physically attacked: the drawings were displayed, unframed and unguarded, in the basement, where they were ripped and defaced. Miró's friend and fervent defender Gasch wrote in his biography fifty years later, "one minor painter, whose name I do not wish to recall and who has long been forgotten, stood in front of the paintings all day long telling anyone prepared to listen that those canvases were the works of a true madman." And that enmity took root: I remember an impromptu talk, one Sunday morning in the mid-1950's at the Sala Pinacoteca, where the painter Puig-dengolas, ignoring the subject of conversation, took hold of the copy of *La Vanguardia* lying on the table, with a photograph of Miró on the cover, and drew two enormous ass's ears on it, which everyone present found terribly amusing.

Apart from Miró's friends Junoy and Llorens Artigas, the critics' comments were uniformly bad. And sales, practically nil. Only one item was sold: the painter Josep Mompou bought *Still Life with Coffee Grinder* for 250 pesetas. The positive lesson Miró learned thanks to Dalmau's generosity and courage was "how tremendously provocative and irritating something as apparently innocuous as painting can be." This discovery remained engraved in his memory, and from that moment on he ceased to accentuate aggressiveness. He declared himself immune to the attacks of his critics, thanks to his firm conviction that he was destined for great things. The attacks even stimulated him further, and I suspect that the friendship that developed between Miró and Gasch stemmed largely from the time when Gasch displayed a Cubist drawing by Miró in the Spring Exhibition of 1919, and it had caused a policeman such hilarity that he had pointed at it as if it were a fairground freak.

Still life with coffee grinder, 1918.

Gasch sided with Miró and cemented a rocklike solidarity between two champions of the avant-garde assailed by the asses and tyrants of academicism.

The rest of that year was also intense, for not only did the reviews *Arc Voltaic* and *Trossos* reproduce Miró drawings on their covers, but on 11 May the artist presented several paintings at the collective exhibition staged by the Courbet group at the Municipal Spring Exhibition. This group of young creators who were determined to combat academicism and bring about an artistic revolution had just been founded by Llorens Artigas, Domingo, Ràfols, Ricart, Sala and Miró himself. The name had been proposed by Llorens Artigas, who told me that it had no political

Cover of the magazine *Arc Voltaic* (1918).

overtones and still less any aesthetic connotations: "Simply because it was short and sounded good." But the group did not last long or leave much mark, for the following year most of its members left for Paris and it dissolved. With the end of the 'Great War', the doors were opened again for the pilgrimage all artists considered an obligatory duty: Paris was the obsession of a whole generation.

It is true that Miró felt a great curiosity to explore Paris and discover for himself everything he had read and heard about the art capital of the world: but it is no less true that he had the personal conviction that, moreover, Paris would understand his so very personal manner of interpreting reality through painting. He decided to apply for a visa from the French Consulate, a formality which in the immediate post-war years was neither quick nor simple. Patience was called for. At the same time, he began to prepare the more prosaic and, for him, detestable, details relating to his maintenance. And the most unpleasant facet was money. He confessed in a letter to Ricart that "of the capital I saved from my wages as a clerk, I only have 25 or 30 pesetas left (I spent the rest on materials and the studio); now I have to admit that my 'fortune' has slipped away, and I have asked my mother for money, to my own great displeasure." It is not hard to perceive the firmness of Miró's decision to take on the Parisian adventure, which had led him to swallow his pride and ask his family for help – although it is noticeable that he attacked its weakest flank. While waiting to travel to France, he painted ceaselessly, especially shut away in Mont-roig during the long summer, determined to capture in the smallest detail the grandeur of the smallest and simplest things. "The calligraphy of a tree or a roof, leaf by leaf, twig by twig, blade by blade and tile by tile (...) Next winter, the critics will continue to say that I persist in my disorientation," he wrote to Ricart. In another letter to him, he acknowledged that "I have not been able to finish one picture (...) This calligraphy business is very time-consuming." Similarly, he wrote to Ràfols, "The joy of coming to understand

33

one blade of grass in a landscape – Why scorn it? Grass as graceful as a tree or a mountain." In another, later, letter to Ricart, he wrote in capitals the magic name, like a password, with the fervent wish that it would produce the desired effects: PARIS, PARIS, PARIS.

Finally, at the end of February 1920, he reached his goal, Paris. At last! He stepped off the train and presented an image which was recorded years later by Ricart in his memoirs: "tubby, Teutonic, ruddy-faced, in a bowler hat and with two large suitcases, an umbrella and walking stick poking out of them, and if one of them was a retrospective poem of a stage-coach novel, the other (made of canvas with riveted leather edges, and seemingly incapable of containing the expansive force it held) was the sort that clowns use all over the world, and it gave him a touching air of a circus performer." He was not alone on his arrival, because he was met on the platform by Llorens Artigas, who by now was an expert in moving around the city. He took Miró straight to the Hôtel de Rouen, in Rue Notre-Dame-des-Victoires. It was a pleasant place to stay, partly because it was very close to where the Count de Lautréamont had lived, and partly because the owner's son-in-law was a Catalan and a generous type: he charged them an almost symbolic rate for the room and invited them to lunch on Sundays, which, with their strictly limited means, took on enormous importance. Another lodger was a young Catalan journalist called Josep Pla. Many Catalans were moving to Paris in those days, but Miró's intention was not to cohabit with them but to go his own way, although it was one thing to be with his friends Ràfols or Ricart and another to be with the likes of Togores, Folch i Torres, Mercadé, Espinalt, Ynglada or Domingo.

The first thing he did, as Victoria Combalia has revealed in her magnificent book on that period, was to visit Picasso, who was then living at Rue de la Boëtie, 23. Although the two artists' mothers knew each other and used to exchange visits, Miró felt such respect for the Andalusian master, 15 years his elder, and such admiration for all of his work, that he had not dared to approach him on the occasion of the pre-mière of *Parade* at the Liceu in Barcelona, which Picasso had attended as the creator of the stage sets. But just before leaving for Paris, he went to see Picasso's mother to ask if she wanted him to take any-thing for her son. "She was remarkable, just like him," Miró told me, "with very lively eyes. She showed me a picture on his bedroom wall that he had drawn just with soap while shaving. She asked me to take him a cake she had made." Miró's mother was the aunt of Picasso's friend and future secretary Jaume Sabartés, as Miró told Melià: "My Aunt Magdalena was a little, bent-over old lady and my mother made me go and visit her very often. I was very young. Picasso had painted a portrait of Sabartés that Aunt Magdalena had in her house. That painting was my first sight of Picasso's work." All of this was favourable to the meet-ing between the two artists. Picasso was delighted to meet Miró, and welcomed him like a younger brother. In a letter to Ràfols on 2 March, Miró wrote: "This morning I went with Ricart to Picasso's house. He received us very warmly in his workshop; we saw what he was making, and he showed us a lot of sculp-tures of Negro art and two canvases by Rousseau." A letter to Dalmau in mid-April shows that he repeated the visit: "I went back to Picasso's house, with the Mompous; he gave us a warm welcome and told us off for not visiting him more often! He was very interested in seeing some of my work. I told him I didn't have anything, that I had it all shut up in boxes. (...) He showed us everything he had and some folders full of drawings. He's a magnificent painter."

But not everything was the colour of roses. Miró enrolled as a free student of drawing at the famous Grande Chaumière school, but it did not take him long to realise he was incapable of working, because he felt paralysed both mentally and physically. It is no surprise that he felt as if he had been knocked out of the fight, a simile which, as we will see later, I think he would have found very accurate. Arriving for the first time in a capital the size of Paris, finding himself face to face with the great works of the history of art, visiting galleries, meeting artists and writers, and all of this without ever having travelled beyond the Barcelona area, Mallorca and Mont-roig, without even having been to the Prado Museum – it is understandable that his sensitive nature should suffer this apparently unexpected reaction. Fortunately he did not give up hope, but attempted to take the fullest advantage of being in Paris, thanks partly to Dalmau's recommendations but particularly to those of Llorens Artigas. He soaked up the post-war atmosphere and the revolutionary reaction of the Dadaists; he spent his mornings visiting the Louvre and other museums, like the Rodin or the Luxembourg, or collections like the Camondo; in the afternoons he toured the galleries, seeing a Picasso exhibition at the Paul Rosenberg Gallery and a retrospective on Odilon Redon. The impact on him was enormous, due to both the quality and quantity of art works he was seeing day after exhausting day. Although Ricart know him well, he could not resist recounting in detail in his memoirs that "walking around the Louvre with him, it was difficult to make conversation: he expressed himself through the sparkle in his eyes and little squeaks of admiration before an important work." Ricart concluded his comments by mentioning that Miró was more hermetic each day. Walking around the colossal stage setting composed by that unique urban landscape, his attention was captured by the entrances to the Métro, designed by the Modernist artist Hector Guimard, which reminded him of Gaudí's works in Barcelona and their influence on him; and he admitted that the arrows and flying birds that appeared in his works originated from the impact caused on him by that discovery.

PICASSO: "YOU HAVE TO JOIN THE QUEUE"

On 26 May he attended the incredible Dada festival held at the Salle Gaveau, which stunned and dazzled him and powerfully confirmed the intuitions he had felt in Barcelona thanks to what he had seen and the contacts he had made at the Dalmau Galleries. This is the impression recorded by the feared writer Maurice Sachs in his formidable chronicle *Au temps de boeuf sur le toit*: "The event was chaired by Fraenckel, Éluard, Soupault and Breton. Cratefuls of poor-quality carrots, turnips, cabbages and oranges were thrown over them. The journalists were shouting and screaming like madmen. (…) Gide said that Cubism is constructive and Dada destructive." I think the impulsiveness that was hatching inside Miró contained a touch of anarchism, which coupled well with the personality and intentions of the Dadaists. I believe that to the end of his days he remained faithful to a style and a commitment that he was beginning to glimpse in those days. This is confirmed by a letter he sent to Ràfols: "I prefer the nonsenses of Picabia or of any other crazy Dadaist to the 'commodities' of my compatriots in Paris, thieving from Renoir (who only has classical value now) or making a watered-down mixture of Sunyer or Matisse. I detest the 'sleeping spirits'". And in mid-June he returned to Barcelona.

On his return, the 'paralytic' of Paris began to feel – thanks to Picasso, the Cubists and the Tarragona countryside – a tremendous urge to set to work. At the same time, he became aware, by comparison, of the true cultural and artistic pulse beating in Barcelona, which led him to confess in despair to his friend Ricart that an artist had to go to Paris as a fighter, not as a mere spectator, and that in any case "I prefer being a failure in Paris to surviving in the stagnant waters of Barcelona," and added, "Decidedly, no more Barcelona-Paris and the countryside, until I die." The harsh but varied landscape of Montroig worked its magical spell on him once again, and became an essential element of his work of that time. He sensed that an irresistible energy that flowed out of the earth and up through his feet, as he expressed it, was now communicating to him all of the inspiration that had been denied to him months earlier. He worked like a man possessed, without stopping, in exhausting days of seven or eight hours. And he wrote to Dalmau that he was starting to paint *La masia* (*The Farm*). It is worth giving the date, because no date as early as this had been quoted until Santos Torroella discovered this letter: 18 July 1920. Miró had realised that his principal mission consisted in materialising his vision in the most localistic form possible, although with a transcendental outlook: in a word, he aimed to become a 'universal Catalan.'

And so, having announced his condemnation of his home town and the local artistic community and the recovery of his capacity to express himself visually, Miró decided to return to Paris, with the aim of settling there for good. This entailed certain prosaic problems such as money, as he commented to his 'confessor,' Ricart: "I want to live as soon as possible without needing my allowance from the family, which I find repugnant. I'll have enough with the cost of the journey and my expenses for surviving in Paris for a couple of months, and after that I'll get by." His idea was to persuade Dalmau to organise an exhibition for him in Paris, as he thought that this would be sufficient to score a success and so become known and climb to the top of the artistic world – his ambitions in this respect never knew any limitations. He put his proposal to Dalmau, who discussed it with Josep Manyac, who had been Picasso's first dealer in Paris and had now inherited the family's safe-making business, with a Surrealist-style shop in Carrer Ferran designed by Jujol. The agreement was signed immediately by means of the purchase of all of the paintings for 1,000 pesetas. And early in February 1921 Miró returned to Paris.

The first thing he had to do was look for a studio, so he went straight to talk to his friend Llorens i Artigas. And he was in luck, because Papitu offered him the temporary possibility of using the studio of the Catalan sculptor Pau Gargallo, who had closed it up for the winter after being appointed director of the Barcelona Artistic Trades School. The only condition was that Miró would have to vacate the studio in the summer. Once more Llorens i Artigas had come to Miró's aid, and he guided him through the labyrinth of the Paris art world. The studio was in Rue Blomet, and Miró rented a room nearby, in the Hôtel Innova, at Boulevard Pasteur, 32; it was a bug-infested dive, but it was good enough as a place to sleep. Gargallo's mother introduced Miró to the surly concierge, knowing the importance of being on good terms with those all-powerful women.

Joan Miró and Papitu Llorens Artigas, two great friends, two great artists.

The second thing to do was to visit Picasso, another 'introducer' although in higher circles. Like the previous year, Miró had again gone to ask Picasso's mother if she wanted him to take anything to her son; she had given him an *ensaïmada* (a Mallorcan pastry) which Miró now hastened to take to Picasso's house in Rue de la Boëtie. Picasso was not at home, but on 14 February he wrote Miró a note of thanks. Miró went to see him shortly afterwards, and when he commented that making one's way in the art world was very difficult, Picasso frankly replied, "Listen, Miró, it's like catching a bus, you have to wait in line, and when it's your turn, you jump on." Picasso did not brush Miró off nor try to get out of helping him: on the contrary, on 25 March Miró wrote to Dalmau that Picasso had come to see him at his studio in Rue Blomet. The master had finally seen the youngster's work and realised that he had talent – and the conviction that Miró could become a real painter is what led Picasso to help him, more than mere friendship. He told the dealers Rosenberg and Kahnweiler about the young Catalan artist.

The most important thing, for the moment, was that Dalmau had kept his word and managed to organise an exhibition for Miró: on 29 April it opened at the Galerie La Licorne and remained open until 14 May. The exhibition was presented by none other than Maurice Raynal, whom Miró had met in Barcelona during the war. Miró hurried to tell his patron, Dalmau, about the event: "Finally we have opened the exhibition. I'm very happy with the *vernissage*. Important representatives from the art world were there, and everyone was very interested. In the morning, when we were hanging pictures, a gentleman arrived at Picasso's recommendation, and he asked the price of the chicken, the console and the Spanish letters. He has not come back." Other visitors were the critic and dealer Paul Guillaume, along with Paul Rosenberg and his brother Léonce, also a dealer. But the overall outcome of the launch was an undeniable failure in terms of sales, even though the few critical comments published were generally favourable. Miró was overcome by an inevitable and comprehensible sensation of defeat. He wrote to Dalmau, "All of my colleagues here are getting ahead: Ricart, Mercadé, Togores (who is now '*classé*') – but the contradiction is that I, who everyone says am destined to succeed and am the best painter of us all, I am just like before, behind a lot of people who are inferior to me."

A few days before moving into Gargallo's studio, Miró had gone to see Max Jacob, to whom he had been introduced by Dalmau. Jacob had suggested meeting at the Café de la Savoyarde, in Montmartre, instead of his sordid room at Rue Gabriel 17. Also present was André Masson, who years later related the meeting in this original fashion: "Joan Miró is as unknown as I am. Miró tells me he's a painter. I tell him I am, too. I tell him I'm moving to Montmartre because I've just rented a studio at Rue Blomet 45. He replies, 'That's odd. I've just rented a studio in the same place.' We're going to be neighbours. A curious meeting. It all seems to be providential." Shortly afterwards, Miró discovered that he was separated by his new neighbour by a simple party wall, so thin that he felt he was actually living with the Masson family, which was none too pleasant. He told me, "They were very noisy. Masson lived with his wife Odette (who he had married in Ceret, with Manolo Hugué as his best man) and their daughter Lili. They had these ferocious arguments, with impressive regularity. They lived in total disorder and filth. I loved that little girl and how she enjoyed riding on my knees. We liked drinking, chatting and listening to music. As if that weren't enough, opposite us there was a hotel full of Algerians, a rowdy lot who organised some almighty brawls that often ended up with someone stabbed. I had to make a great effort to concentrate on my work. Masson went through some very hard times, and before getting his contract with Kahnweiler he had to resign himself to correcting proofs for the *Journal Officiel*."

He described the studio in Rue Blomet to me as "wretched, dismal; it had nothing, not even furniture. I had limited myself to buying a stove for just 45 francs at the Marché aux Puces, a divan, a chair and nothing else. The window panes were broken and I had no money to replace them. The stove wouldn't light even when I had coal. They were tough times." He cleaned the place himself, naturally, and even waxed the wooden floor. Before long the place looked clean and tidy. The walls were an immaculate white, his paintings were carefully turned to the wall and stacked according to size, while his spotless paint brushes and tubes were kept in rigorous alignment. The most attractive feature of the studio was a delightful, evocative inner patio with a lovely lilac tree that was extolled in a poem by Robert Desnos. Some years later, when the building had been demolished and Malraux was Minister of Culture, Miró offered to install a sculpture there in honour of the dead poet, with the poem engraved by his own hand. And now Miró's *Moon Bird* has pride of place there. It was Desnos who was responsible for making fashionable the Bal Nègre dance sessions organised in the back room of the corner café, having dedicated to them one of his articles on 'squashed dogs' that he published in *L'Intransigeant,* as a result of which the dances maintained their intoxicating rhythms but lost the aroma of the snake-hipped Martinicans and filled up with white snobs instead.

Picasso's influence paid dividends. Miró received a visit from Paul Rosenberg, who arrived puffing and panting and more than a little annoyed at having to climb five floors. But he was not interested in the works Miró showed him. The same thing happened with Kahnweiler, who came shortly afterwards, having previously rejected Masson's request to visit him. Masson, who was kind and generous, had also pressured Jacques Doucet to examine Miró's work, but Doucet so disliked what he saw that he told Masson, "Your neighbour is mad!" Picasso's efforts were inspired by something more than the simple, fervent desire to help a young Barcelona colleague, as is confirmed by the fact that he acquired two of Miró's paintings and kept them until his death. During the exhibition at La Licorne, Picasso had told Dalmau how much he admired the self-portrait *Young Man in a Red Shirt*, and Miró, wanting to win his favours, gave it to him, which pleased Picasso a great deal. The gallery was losing money and closed down before long; its owner, Doctor Girardin, who was also a collector, not having sold a single picture, decided to buy all of them from Dalmau, through Miró's exclusive dealer, Pierre Loeb. One day Picasso went to ask the price of *Spanish Dancer*, and bought it; Loeb reported the event to Miró, saying "Do you know who's bought the *Dancer*? Picasso! He's done it to laugh at us!" Miró insisted on telling me the story in detail, because he was determined I should know that at that time – the year 1926 – even Loeb did not truly believe in Miró's art. But business, ah, that was a different matter.

Miró's time at Rue Blomet proved vital not only for forming good relationships, but particularly for his artistic development. Masson introduced him to a series of figures, mainly poets, who were destined to imprint character on him, such as Pierre Reverdy, Tristan Tzara, Georges Limbour, Armand Salacrou, Antonin Artaud, Michel Leiris, Roland Tual and Robert Desnos himself. It is important to recall that, as Masson said, poetry in its widest sense was an essential element, for both he and Miró had set out to be painter-poets in search of a plastic language that would transcend simple painting, that would *go further*. From the very beginning Miró recognised that this was the world that interested him, and that the type of intellectual exchange and cultural enrichment he needed was not to be gained from the theorising painters, whom he hated. From then on he began to title his works in French, a language which he now used constantly in his tasks of intellectual reflection, though he continued to write his notes normally in Catalan. In his later years, he acknowledged this reality when interviewed by his biographer, Jacques Dupin: "Rue Blomet was a decisive moment. There I discovered everything that I am. Firstly it was friendship, exchange of ideas and exalted discovery through a group of marvellous friends (...) We argued, we drank a lot – this was the time of eau-de-vie with water, and the 'Curaçao mandarins.' They used to go there on the Métro, on the famous North-South, that connected Montmartre with the Rive Gauche."

At the beginning of this book I described how Miró began *The Farm* in Mont-roig. This is a grandiose work, not only in its unusually large size, but as an inventory of the rural world that Miró absorbed so intensely every summer, and even more so as a synthesis of his visual universe at that time: the countryside seen through the poetic eyes of a city dweller. Once he finished it, instead of trying to recreate it in subsequent works – a road that leads straight to mannerism – he would opt to make a break. To achieve that goal, shut away in his solitude, since his parents were not there, and by the light of a carbide lamp, he decided to pay tribute to the legendary landscape in which he found himself immersed. He would unfurl all of the ceremonial liturgy: he would plant his easel under the lofty blue sky, in front of the house, and copy all the things he saw before him, even if he had to place them there himself, like the stool or the cart or the little boy, who was by no means the *caganer* ('shitter') figure mentioned by Robert Hughes in one of his frequent arbitrary comments. He painted the giant eucalyptus or the tiny ant with the same fondness and precision. It took two years: he developed the painting in Barcelona and finished it off in Rue Blomet. So it is no surprise that, in order not to lose the 'thread' of the setting, he went so far as to go to the Bois de Boulogne to pick herbs and copy them in the foreground. But they were 'false' and did not inspire him, so he asked the family to send him herbs from Mont-roig, a ceremony which is not hard to understand. "They arrived all dried up, but they enabled me to go on with my work," he told me. He also told me that he had spent so long on that picture, trying to capture that reality with total precision, that every time he realised he was deviating from the model, as had occurred with the eucalyptus, "I erased what I had drawn with a piece of chalk like children use on the blackboard at school, and I made the necessary corrections." This anti-virtuosity, far from being a mark of inferiority, and even though he was not aware of it at the time, was a blessing that added to the intensity of the result.

Once the painting was duly completed, the adventure of selling it began, and it is worth relating in detail. First Miró took it to Guillaume. Then he took it to the prestigious Gustave Coquiot, who displayed it for one whole day at the Le Jockey café in Montparnasse and presented it in person; here it was seen by Schwanchenberger, an individual who always wore a tailcoat and was interested in the Catalan painters. Miró even wrote to the eminent Barcelona collector Plandiura, who did not even bother to reply. All Miró's efforts were in vain. Léonce Rosenberg, a gallery owner and the editor of *L'Effort Moderne*, exhibited it at the Autumn Salon, but the press dedicated less than a dozen lines to it. Having promised Picasso his help, Rosenberg kept the picture for a couple of months, but on seeing how hard it was to sell, and reasoning that apartments were getting smaller and smaller, he suggested cutting it into eight pieces and selling them separately. Despite so many failures, and the fact that every time Miró had to transport it he had to spend his meagre food money on a taxi and also run the risk of damaging it, he refused to lower his sails, such was the faith he had in the picture.

BOXING WITH HEMINGWAY

It was the crazy American poet Evan Shipman, a great
gambler and horse-racing fan who could be rich one
minute and flat broke the next, who succumbed to
the enchantment of *The Farm* in an instant of passion
while it was displayed at the Galerie Pierre; he
obtained the first purchase option on it and the possibility of paying in instalments of 5,000 francs after
bargaining with the manager Jacques Viot, on the
condition that the painting would only be handed
over once the sum total was paid. Shipman then discovered that his friend Ernest Hemingway liked the
painting a lot, but the novelist was as broke as Miró
himself. When it came to the moment of truth, Shipman had found someone prepared to pay four times
the asking price for it, but he preferred Hemingway
to have it. The dispute was settled in a way close to the
heart of that inveterate gambler: the two candidates
threw dice for the painting, and Hemingway won. Let
us allow the writer himself to unfold the ending, in
his own particular style: "When the last instalment fell
due, the dealer arrived and said he had no money at
home nor in the bank, and if I didn't pay the amount
that same day he would keep the painting. Finally,
Dos Passos, Shipman and I went begging for money
around several bars and restaurants, we went to get

the painting and brought it home in a taxi. In the open taxi the wind caught the big canvas as though it were a sail, and we made the taxi driver crawl along. When we arrived home, we hung the picture on the wall and felt as happy as sandboys. I wouldn't change it for any other painting in the world. I had a visit from Miró, and he told me, 'I'm very happy it's you who's got *The Farm*'." Subsequently, Hemingway gave the picture to his wife Hadley, and shortly before her death she left it to the MOMA in New York.

Hemingway, Shipman and Ezra Pound dedicated a special issue of the New York *Little Review* to Miró, specifying that he was a Catalan. "Masson had introduced me to Hemingway. He took an interest in my work straight away," Miró told me. "We became friends and saw each other regularly. At that time he lived in Rue Notre-Dame-des-Champs. He was warm, friendly, and as poor as me. And to earn money he worked as a sparring partner for heavyweight boxers. We used to go to the gym at the American Centre, in the Boulevard Raspail, where we took boxing lessons. I used to do sports too: it helped me to keep fit and to have a clear head for my work, which absorbed me completely. Sometimes I sparred with Hemingway." I remarked to Miró that Man Ray, in his memoirs, said that when none of the writers' friends wanted to spar with him he would pick Miró. "That's not how it was," Miró told me. "I boxed with him the same as the others did. He could hit, he could hit hard; but not me, of course. We made an amusing couple, him so big and strong and me so small. Around the ring, a bunch of queers used to enjoy watching us. That amused Hemingway no end." Morley Callaghan, a young Canadian writer who was a good boxer and occasionally used the gym, said that Miró was also called on to referee a few bouts between him and Hemingway. He said Miró's total lack of knowledge of English was frankly no help, but it did not stop him from eagerly assuming the responsibility and shouting "Stop!" every three minutes and ensuring the breaks between rounds never went beyond exactly one minute. That friendship with Hemingway lasted for many years: he invited him to Barcelona, accommodated him and his wife in Mallorca, and naturally took him to Mont-roig – Hemingway had the tower of the farmhouse copied on a larger scale for the house he had built in Havana – and the two men also met again during Miró's long stay in New York in 1947.

Miró's life was by now structured with an inflexible rigidity, and he always maintained that style, since what most interested and satisfied him was to work, work, work, whether in his studio or simply reading, thinking, reflecting, taking notes for future projects. The only interruptions were his travels. He knew himself well, and was fully aware that he needed to follow a strict routine in order to be productive, in view of his total lack of ability to express himself visually. He did not take long to realise that he worked much less in Paris than in Mont-roig or Barcelona, where there was no-one to bother him. Just as during Mr. Civil's art classes he had learned the initiatic ritual of cleaning and ordering all of his drawing and painting tools, now, in an ever more complete and radical manner, he was coming to realise that he needed to impose order on his life to facilitate his work and concentration. And so he accustomed himself to leading a very tightly-ordered life. During his stay in

Mont-roig he did a lot of exercise, not only swimming a lot but also doing Swedish gymnastics.

Before long he realised that order combined with a little daily exercise was very good for him, toning his body, clearing his mind and stimulating his spirit. This was the reason why he took to boxing during his penniless times in Paris, perhaps under the influence of Hemingway. He had not started there, though, but in Barcelona or perhaps Mont-roig. In 1918 he regularly went to the Club Marítim in the Barceloneta district, where he skipped rope, did Swedish gymnastics routines and, especially, swam. He took good care of his figure, and if he saw a bit of a paunch developing he immediately set about getting rid of it, by means of long runs along the beach, well wrapped up to sweat as much as possible. In 1922, in a letter to Tual, he described his life in Mont-roig: "During my leisure hours I lead a primitive existence. Almost naked, I do exercise, I run like a madman and I skip rope. At night, when I finish work, I swim in the sea. I'm convinced that serious personal work only begins with maturity, and to attain this point of growth you have to lead a healthy life (...) I don't see anyone, and my chastity is absolute." He wanted to get fit and stay that way, no matter what. I think this obsession, which he maintained as long as age permitted, had its origins in his childhood illness, when he came close to death. In fact, I suspect that he dedicated these efforts to physical exercise and healthy living not so much to postpone death as to avoid falling into depression, that fearful prospect for him.

And if Miró wanted order in everything to do with his work, and if he wanted his body to maintain the same physical order, then his external appearance also had to display the same rhythm and balance. Immediately after finishing each gruelling working day, he washed meticulously, combed and brushed his hair and put on a sober suit that he associated with British elegance, as his friend Gasch remembered him. The young boxer-writer Callaghan says that Miró wore a black hat, a fashionable shirt and a smart businessman's suit, with a carefully combed and fixed fringe across his forehead. He told Dupin that he wore soft spats and sometimes even a monocle. Was he imitating Tzara? Whatever the truth, this was more than a passing fad. Even when penniless, something inside him prohibited him from showing the slightest external self-neglect. He needed to feel confident and dominant in his surroundings.

Each summer he had to leave the studio and hand it back to Gargallo. He would have done so anyway, because he needed to return to Mont-roig. This he did every June, even when he had his own studio. He moved into the farmhouse for the summer solstice and stayed until the harvest. Then he moved on to Barcelona, for stays of irregular duration. In this way he established a routine which alternated a period of cultural stimulation in Paris with the counterpoint of absolute concentration in Mont-roig and contact with his homeland, Catalonia. In the countryside he led a monastic life which he only interrupted to sit down at the table with his parents or to eat the meals prepared by the tenant farmer's wife, and to take exercise by running or swimming. In Mont-roig he felt the physical pleasure of touching the earth with his feet and feeling the energy that entered through them and rose up through his legs, as if he were a tree. It was for this reason that he said that in order to leap into the air, referring to a challenging artistic change, the vital thing was to have one's feet firmly planted on the ground. He confirmed to Gasch that "Where I am happiest is in Catalonia, I think the pure Catalan is in Tarragona (…) All my life has been conceived in Mont-roig, everything I've done in Paris has been conceived in Mont-roig, not thinking of Paris, which I detest." Secluded in Mont-roig, he found the peace and relaxation needed by his peculiar manner of working, so slow, painstaking, ordered, to mature in steady steps and according to the detailed plan he had laid out with a lot of time, rigour and attention to detail. And one day he summed up his ambition to create a work with very local profiles, but with the aim of becoming a 'universal Catalan,' in these unequivocal terms: "I don't feel any kinship with the rest of the Spanish people. I feel Catalan. I visit Spain like a foreign country, as if I were travelling to Holland. But I do feel an affinity with French culture. In Mont-roig I'm at home, not in Madrid, nor Seville, nor Cordoba. I like them a lot, but it's something different."

When he went back to Paris in the winter of 1922, he recovered the studio in Rue Blomet, but he rented another room, this time in the Hôtel Haute Loire, at Boulevard Raspail, 203. The following year he also had to comply with the agreement with Gargallo, but now he rented a furnished apartment at Rue Berthelot, 10. At this point he was able to move permanently into the Rue Blomet studio. He was coming to realise that he was more comfortable with the poets to whom Masson introduced him than with those artists who intellectualised painting; in this way, he became close friends with figures like Leiris, Desnos, Éluard and Aragon. He was a tireless and inquisitive reader, not only of his friends' poetry but also of Rimbaud, Lautréamont, Baudelaire and Apollinaire, who he never managed to meet. He was also greatly influenced, but in a very different way, by Jarry. At the beginning, understandably, the interest in reading these authors was surpassed by that of listening attentively to their endless discussions on poetry sitting around a café table or in Masson's house – every time someone interesting arrived, Masson would alert Miró with a couple of bangs on the dividing wall.

As a result of these experiences and of the intention, shared with Masson, of transcending painting through the gateway opened up by poetry, Miró came to abandon the themes and even the style that culminated in *The Farm* and to undertake a solitary adventure, virtually in the dark. It is significant to note that later on he became close friends with René Char, who wrote "*Il faut marcher le front contre la nuit,*" the best synthesis, in my opinion, of an avant-gardist attitude. It was for this reason that Miró did not later fall into the temptation of wandering into that wasteland that was defined as "painting-painting."

Work, work, work – that was all very well, but what could Miró do to amuse himself if he never had any money? One day he told me very expressively: "Another of my ways of relaxing was to go out walking. Yes, I enjoyed walking. It was cheap … and while I was walking I thought about my work, I meditated. Masson and I used to go out a lot with Max Jacob. Jacob had just converted to Catholicism and was going through a stage of powerful devotions. He used to tell us to meet him at the Sacré Coeur church at seven in the morning when he came out of communion! Then the three of us would go for a walk. Jacob invited his friends to the Café de la Savoyarde opposite the church. The view was attractive: from the terrace you could see that fantastic panorama of Paris." Masson, for his part, confirmed this: "Max Jacob lived in a dungeon in Rue Gabrielle. But Max Jacob had a *salon!* And that *salon* was La Savoyarde."

They also frequented the Café de la Rotonde, which had just been enlarged after the war and where it was hard to find a seat between five in the evening and the early morning. Miró told me that he used to ask for a *café crème* because it was the cheapest drink on the list; what he consumed in immense proportions was information and new items of interest. But he was not the type to spend all his time in the cafés, because the most important thing for him was to continuing working in his studio, which cost him a good deal of sweat and tears. When he had money, he allowed himself some pleasure as a reward: "I was always starving," he told me, "and whenever I had money I went to the Restaurant des Mille Colonnes in Rue de la Gaité. If I had more money, I allowed myself the luxury of going to a more expensive one in the same street – Papitu often went there, he had more money than me. Sometimes I had dinner at Au Nègre de Toulouse, where Joyce went almost every day. He introduced me to Hemingway. He was a strange type, he spoke very little, and he was always accompanied by his daughter, who acted as his secretary because his eyesight was very poor. I regularly went to the bookshop Shakespeare & Co. – Hemingway once brought Sylvia Beach, the owner, to my workshop." In 1922, Sylvia Beach had published *Ulysses*, the novel that raised Joyce to the Olympus of world literature.

The way of avoiding the temptation of restaurants was to cook at home. Miró had no idea about cooking, but he gradually learned, thanks to the lessons of the farmer's wife at Mont-roig, who also showed him how to make a bed. She was the same woman who appeared in the paintings *The Farm* and *The Farmer's Wife*, the mother of the four-year-old girl who posed as the model for *Portrait of a Little Girl*.

In the same way as he had occasionally gone to the West Indian dances that Desnos made fashionable, he also got to know, through Iliazd, the Russian dances held at Bullier, just opposite the famous Closerie des Lilas, the headquarters of the now ailing Juan Gris, who Miró had met at Masson's house. It was no surprise that Miró felt unable to go out on the dance floor. And not because he was too shy, by no means – he had no idea of how to do the steps of the dances or how to follow a rhythm. He reached the conclusion that knowing how to dance formed part of the culture of a young person of his ambitions. We have already seen that Miró was always smartly dressed, but now his friends began to notice that on certain days he vanished from sight, and one afternoon one of his friends happened to spot him in the street, dressed even more elegantly than usual. They decided to find out Miró's secret, convinced that he was having an affair with a woman. So they followed him, and to their great surprise they saw Miró go into a dance school and place himself in the arms of a man – a male dancing teacher! I was told this story one day by Papitu Llorens i Artigas.

None of them had two pennies to rub together, but they had fun together and they were happy, enormously happy. Another figure Miró met at that time was Henry Miller, to whom Hemingway introduced him, as he did John Dos Passos. In his room at the Villa Seurat, Miller had hung a sign saying "*La maison ne fait pas de crédit.*" He was so poor he did not even have a stove, and he confessed to his protector and lover Anaïs Nin that he wrote *Tropic of Cancer* wrapped up in a dressing gown, overcoat and scarf. Unforgettable days – and so, when Miller wrote the story *The Smile at the Foot of the Stairs,* he stated that the staircase and the moon constituted his tribute to his friend Miró, as a memory of the first of Miró's paintings he ever saw, the *Dog Barking at the Moon,* which also included a staircase. This was what gave me the idea, in 1966, when Edicions Proa was preparing to publish a hand-composed but budget-priced edition of Joan Oliver's Catalan translation of the story, to ask Miró to illustrate the book cover; which he did with great pleasure, and free of charge.

Max Ernst had just painted his group picture *Meeting of Friends,* which portrayed a number of Dadaists and future Surrealists alongside Raphael and Dostoievsky. Miró does not appear in it. He and Ernst had just met but were not yet close. Although cultivating a social life, even in cultural circles, was not Miró's strong suit, he imposed it on himself as an obligation, knowing he needed to find out what was going on, at least concerning art and poetry, but also to weave himself a social network that would allow him to make contacts, since his work was still not known. He made contact with the group of Surrealists established at Rue du Château 54, like Prévert, Péret, Duhamel, Tanguy or Queneau, with whom he played the fashionable new game of *cadavres exquis* ('exquisite corpses'). And, naturally, he met the dictator of

Rue Fontaine, André Breton. At one time, perplexed, he asked Masson, "Who should I go to see, Picabia or Breton?" Masson's reply left no room for doubt: "Picabia is the past, Breton is the future."

The extent to which he formed intense relationships with all kinds of poets is revealed, I think, by the fact that he even became friends with someone as difficult and moody as Ezra Pound. A vestige of this has recently been discovered in a previously unknown correspondence, including this revealing note from 1926: "Dear Miró, where on earth are you? I went to Rue Blomet and they don't know you. Give me a sign of life!"

He felt no need to meet in person artists he admired, as was the case with Klee, who had made a great impact on him since 1923, particularly after he became aware that Klee's work extended beyond painting – but Miró took no steps to make personal contact with him. This respect was mutual: years later, Kandinsky, whose work fascinated Miró, with whom he became a close friend soon after escaping to Paris from Hitler's Germany, told him one day in the Café Cyrano, their regular haunt, that Klee had once said of Miró's paintings, "We'll have to keep an eye on this lad."

It was now 1924, and Miró found himself standing at a crossroads. He had abandoned one style, that of doing 'calligraphy' from a very personal viewpoint, to enter a different, imaginary style in which he was still feeling his way. He had been led along this path through his contact with the world of poetry. For this reason, in the Oriental fashion, he was lured into persevering with poetry, in order to transcend painting by placing on the canvas a letter, a word or even a fragment of a word, like that "sard," which referred to 'sardine,' not to the Catalan dance the *sardana*. It is true that Surrealism helped him, but also that he was more comfortable with Dadaism and particularly with the Dadaists and their youthful, combative, somewhat anarchist spirit, which connected well with his own impulsive personality. He was aware that he was moving into unexplored territory. He was not daunted by the challenge, but he suffered a fear of losing his bearings. He confessed this panic to Ràfols, comparing it to that of a traveller in unknown lands.

He did not need to use stimulants for inspiration: at no time in his life did he feel a need for drink, and even less so for drugs. He had enough with poetry or architecture, being transported by the work of Gaudí in particular. He himself has said that he sought the appropriate atmosphere during his daily walks, or in certain noises, like a horse in a field, cartwheels, footsteps, crickets, animal calls in the night. The spectacle of the night sky entranced him. And just as he rejected all stimulants, he also made no use of dreams, which had become fashionable through Surrealism; he did not, for example, subject himself to hypnotism as Desnos did. Moreover, he declared that he never had any dreams and he slept like a log, like a child. He had enough, then, with his own vitality, spurred on by his work in the studio.

But this was a difficult time for him, as he was constantly penniless and his pride prevented him from asking his parents to send him money or asking his friends for a loan; at times he barely ate, practically fasting, and this caused him hallucinations. He ate only figs and chewed rubber in order to deceive his hunger with the exercise of his jaws. One day when the sculptor Hans Arp was visiting Miró's studio, all there was to eat were turnips with butter.

HUNGER INSPIRES

Miró composed his colossal painting *Harlequinade* with the disciplined exercise of attempting to reflect the hallucinations he suffered on returning home with a ferocious hunger after being unable to have dinner. Then he would sit facing one of the blank walls of the studio and apply himself to capturing on paper the fantastic forms that appeared in his mind, transferring them later to canvas. He told me, "Hunger put me in a kind of trance, like the Orientals experience. Then I would make preparatory sketches of the general outline of the work, to know where I had to put each thing. After meditating a lot on what I aimed to do, I began painting, and I introduced all of the changes I felt appropriate as I went along. It's true that I was very interested in Hieronymus Bosch, but I wasn't thinking of him when I was working on *Harlequinade*. That picture has elements that were repeated later in other works: the staircase, which is escape but also elevation; the animals and especially the insects, which have always interested me a great deal; the dark sphere that appears on the right is a representation of the Earth, because at the time I was obsessed with one idea – I have to conquer the world! And the cat, which was always by my side as I painted. The black triangle in the window represents the Eiffel Tower. I was trying to reach into the magical side of things. For example, the cauliflower has a secret life, and that's what interested me, not its external appearance."

In other words, Miró was by now a painter capable of setting free a whole world of demons that were lurking in his mind, a universe of deranged hallucinations – but the danger, once installed in that world, lay in not knowing how to return from it. I believe that Miró's self-discipline and rigorous routine, plus his sense of elegance, were an invaluable aid to him in not losing sight of reality, in maintaining his orientation and equilibrium. He suffered a lot during this period: he had abandoned the type of painting he knew how to do, he had embarked on a road leading who knew where, his work had not gained the attention of the public, he had no economic resources … in a word, he had no idea how everything might turn out. And if that were not enough, his introverted and incommunicative nature prevented him from seeking allies or giving vent to the doubts and anxieties that tortured him; in this case, his solitude helped to aggravate his situation.

But his strength, resolution and firm conviction in himself and his possibilities enabled him to resist, which did him an enormous amount of good. The fact that he did not fall into depression but instead convinced himself that he could withstand the suffering hardened him and stiffened further his confidence and maturity. At this point he reached the certainty that he was ready to stand up to all the challenges life could throw at him. In later years he acknowledged that this testing time had given him the endurance of a long-distance runner, unlike others who had always had things easy. His middle-class parents often asked him if he needed help, but his answer was always a resounding 'no' – and he never regretted this, in fact he was proud of having always resisted the temptation. He also acknowledged in later life that he had actually been fortunate in not having a dealer at that time, because he suspected that he would have been unable to abandon the more commercial line of *The Farm* to embark on the Surrealism that neither he nor, much less, his potential buyers, were well equipped to accept. He suffered a lot, but he was free, absolutely free, and he took the path his gut feelings indicated to him. Masson and Desnos encouraged him to continue that way; Éluard and Breton, on the other hand, had stared at *The Farm* for a long time but, significantly, they had not made any comment about it.

In any case, Miró did not pay too much attention to Breton, whom he considered a dogmatic extremist. But the theoretician of Surrealism gave an effusive welcome to this powerful new artistic talent. No doubt due to the influence of others, in 1924, Miró, along with Artaud, Masson, Tual and Leiris, agreed to join Breton's group of militants.

That summer Miró once again returned to Montroig in search of the energy it always instilled in him. Here he maintained a direct, emotive relationship with nature, both fauna and flora. He had always been fascinated by animals, and particularly insects like flies and mosquitoes. And this passion was further fuelled by the opportunity to learn about his world in greater detail and rigour, particularly when Breton's wife Simone gave him a book by the French etymologist Jean-Henri Fabre which fascinated him.

"Insects are marvellous," he told me, "and I've always been very interested in them. When I was young I began to paint some in *The Farm* or *Head of a Catalan Peasant*. The praying mantis puts her arms to her head as if she were really praying, and when the mating session is finished she eats the male. A magnificent, beautiful insect." He was also fascinated by trees: "A tree is more than a plant," he used to say, "it is a disconcerting, human thing that has life, that speaks and breathes." He painted the eucalyptus in *The Tilled Field* with an ear and an eye, no doubt influenced by Romanesque art. On the other hand, he was struck by the immobility of a pallet, perhaps because he sought movement in things that did not seem to have any, just as he was drawn to the power of large empty spaces, the eloquence of silence, the "silent music" of St John of the Cross. He could find inspiration in the smallest and most insignificant thing on the face of the earth, whether he discovered it moving in the fields or inert on the sand of the beach. For the moment it was a theme to be materialised; later he would take hold of that form and transform it into a sculpture. "Everything appears in my compositions, whether it is the capricious heads of wild mushrooms or the seventy-seven shapes of the pumpkin." Around that time he told Gasch, "You have to grasp the earth, you have to listen to the cry of the earth ... Paris is all very well, unfortunately you have to pass through Paris ... Madrid, the Prado Museum, all that business of Spanish society, Zurbarán, yes, all of that is all very well, but you have to connect with the earth. For me, a mineralogy museum is something striking ... Everything that comes out of the earth has an immense value. You have to stand on the earth if you want to paint, so that its power enters your body through your feet. When I'm cold, I stand on a straw mat, because that's like the earth, it comes out of the ground. I can't paint in a studio with a linoleum floor: You have to stand on the earth if you want to paint…" And that same simplicity led him to prefer popular art, or a tool carved by a farmer, like a wooden pitchfork.

He returned to Paris from Mont-roig, where he had worked without rest, with fresh works and renewed energies. It did not bother him that Breton and Éluard were disconcerted or that Kahnweiler said the best place for those paintings was the fire. But on 1 April 1925 something fundamental occurred: following an introduction by Evan Shipman, the writer who had been instrumental in the purchase of *The Farm*, Miró signed a contract with Jacques Viot, the manager of the recently-inaugurated Galerie Pierre, owned by Pierre Loeb. Both Viot and Loeb were figures with a certain weight. Miró told me, "Viot was a bold, decisive character, and he said to me 'If Max Ernst can live on 1,500 francs a month, I think you can, too.' And in exchange he took all of my production. That was the first contract I signed in my life. I've still got it." In fact, that amount did not stretch very far, enough to buy canvases and paints and to subsist, but what I think was more significant was the psychological security, that is, the reassurance that someone with a certain prestige believed in his art: that must have meant a lot in those days.

TANGOING WITH A TALLER WOMAN

Viot knew how to organise things, and he proposed doing something more than merely publicising Miró with a range of paintings and drawings, and that was to launch him as a bright new star that was destined to soar irresistibly to the heights of the artistic firmament. So he organised an exhibition for Miró that was to open on 12 June and last for two weeks. This was the least he could do – what really mattered was the rest. And Viot took care of the physical surroundings as much as the intellectual setting. To start with, he commissioned the presentation text from Benjamin Péret, a conspicuous name in Breton's group; and Péret did not write something merely adequate, but a text that still today conserves literary force and aesthetic commitment. The time of the *vernissage* was also original: midnight. Viot created an invitation including the signatures of such important figures in the Surrealist revolution as, in order of appearance on the card: Max Morissen, Theodore Fraenkel, Georges Malkine, Roland Tual, Mathias Lübeck, Pierre Naville, Jacques Baron, Michel Leiris, Roger Vitrac, Paul Éluard, René Crevel, Benjamin Péret, Joe Bousquet, Marcel Noll, J. Camus, Robert Desnos, Philippe Soupault, Antonin Artaud, Georges Limbourg, Jacques André Boiffard, André Breton and

Max Ernst. Such an amalgamation of names means that this event must be interpreted as an official exhibition of the group, even though it was an individual show.

From the social point of view, the event was a great success. There was so much traffic milling around Rue Bonaparte, 13, that the police were called in to prevent chaos. Everyone from the Montparnasse of Youki and Kiki was there, but so too was the heir to the crown of Sweden, Prince Eugene. There were so many visitors that they had to enter in turns, and at one moment there were so many people inside the first-floor establishment that it seemed the floor might cave in. To entertain people waiting in the street, a *cobla* band played *sardanes*, a surprise that Picasso had personally organised for his friend. I cannot resist the temptation to quote Viot's description of the night, which exudes the aroma of the time: "Miró had made an effort of coquetry. He is always concerned about the latest fashion trends, and he has a weakness for wristwatches. That night he had regaled himself in the official style. He wore a blazer, grey trousers and white spats. He was wonderfully polite with everyone, but he was so afraid of committing an oversight that he seemed stricken by anxiety. Afterwards we took him to Montparnasse, and I still have a very vivid memory of something that happened: Miró, looking more worried than ever, dancing a tango with a woman much taller than him. Not one *glissé*, not one figure, not the slightest little step were forgotten. The other dancers had stopped to admire such concentration. And Miró, tense, continued to dance his tango as if he had learned it from a book." Envisaging this spectacle, I can only imagine the envy this would have provoked in Soutine, who, as soon as he began to be famous, enrolled at a dancing school in order to display a minimum of style on the floor, and would have paid the earth to have become a consummate tango dancer!

Another very curious incident was only reported by a Prague newspaper. It said that "The well-known rationalist architect Adolf Loos arrived at the *vernissage* with a sad expression and a sinister air, carrying a pair of scissors he had found in the street. He gave them to the painter Pascin [one of the gallery's artists, having opened there in 1924] and asked him, "Do you like this exhibition?" Pascin, drunk on champagne, stuck the scissors into one of the paintings. But no-one took much notice and the night continued its course."

The exhibition proved to be a success with critics and buyers alike. The original, creative Surrealist Raymond Roussel, so admired by Dalí, confessed to his colleague Leiris that "These works go beyond painting." In a minority-interest cultural magazine, *Le Crapouillot*, I chanced to find the gallery's announcement of the exhibition. The painter's name appeared as 'Joao Miró.' I showed it to him, saying that we all knew he was Catalan but now it seemed he was also capable, if the occasion so required, of passing himself off as Portuguese, and he burst out laughing.

Shortly afterwards, Miró attended the famous tribute to Saint-Pol-Roux, who before taking his afternoon nap used to fix a sign on his study door saying '*Le poète travaille.*' And in a way it may have been true, if we consider what Breton said about the creative use of dreams. The event took place on 13 June of that same year, 1925. Miró himself described it to me as follows: "Michel Leiris, one of the members of the Rue Blomet group, used to organise amusing events. The most famous was a tribute banquet for Saint-Pol-Roux in the restaurant of the Closerie des Lilas. Things gradually hotted up, and Leiris, more excited than ever, began to shout subversive, anti-French slogans like 'Death to France!' A tremendous scuffle soon broke out. Leiris took a real bruising, and his face finished up looking like a map." The yells and slogans had been very varied and even picturesque, like Ernst's 'Long live Germany!' and 'Long live China!', while others even called a toast to the people of the Rif, but Leiris' provocation went too far, and the crowd in the street might have lynched him if it had not been for the police, who came and arrested him but then gave him another beating in the cells. The funniest thing was that Miró also let out a very curious and unexpected cry – 'Down with the Mediterranean!' – directed against the dictatorial academicism and neo-classicism then ruling the art world in Catalonia. Miró thoroughly enjoyed this kind of anti-establishment manifestations, and taking part in them made him feel that Dadaist spirit that had so attracted him and that he attempted to keep alive to the very end.

He was then invited to take part in the collective exhibition presented at the Galerie Pierre, 'Surrealist Painting,' which was an official event of the group. I do not know if Diaghilev visited the exhibition in person, but the fact is that he once again demonstrated his sensibility and intuition by expressing his interest in that kind of art, and it seems that, following Picasso's recommendation, he even bought some pictures by Ernst and Miró which he immediately gave to Serge Lifar. This led to the two artists being commissioned to produce the sets and costumes for the ballet *Romeo and Juliet*. Miró was thrilled by the proposal: back in Barcelona he had been drawn to the world of the theatre in all its forms, from the popular, licentious *café-concerts* of the Paral·lel to the refined Russian Ballet presented at the Liceu in 1917, and he had also once painted a ballerina. I suspect that Gasch's influence lay behind this decisive event. The fact was that the challenge of designing the backdrops and some of the costumes afforded him a new experience in an unexplored field. He was also enormously attracted by the idea of direct contact with the public, which was virtually barred to him as a painter. But he did not imagine that this very contact posed the risk of a mass negative reaction at the moment of presentation of the work. And in this case the scandal was spectacular, although its background was entirely ideological, not artistic.

The date was 18 May 1926, and the place the Théâtre Sarah Bernhardt. The ballet had been premièred a few days earlier in Monte Carlo. In Paris, Breton's tame acolytes had bowed to his dictates: what was needed was a violent condemnation of the servile collaboration of the bourgeoisie in having prostituted themselves to vile capital. They organised a mob trained to ruin the Paris opening with a scandalous protest. As soon as the opening curtain went up, they scattered a shower of fliers proclaiming, in red ink, a text signed by Breton and Aragon which began like this: "It is inadmissible for thought to be at the service of money." The curtain was brought down immediately. Aragon, leaning over the balcony of a box, insulted the audience, while the rest of the group yelled, howled, screamed and sounded klaxons. The uproar was deafening, and there was even considerable pushing and shoving: Lady Abby snatched a protester's trumpet and trampled on it, but its owner yanked at her corset and left her half naked. The police charged in and arrested some of the protesters. And when the audience reacted by applauding and demanding the resumption of the ballet, there still remained a few boycotters to shout "Shit!" Another pleasure Miró derived from *Romeo and Juliet* was its presentation at Barcelona's Gran Teatre del Liceu on 13 May 1927, providing him with a hometown triumph that had been denied until then. But he was no doubt saddened by the fact that it could not be witnessed by the father who had never shown confidence in him: he had died in Mont-roig less than a year earlier, on 9 July 1926.

Miró's standing among the Surrealists was subsequently restored thanks to the publication of a text written by Éluard, but in reality he had never given himself to that revolution in heart and soul, and had even marked out a certain distance from it, being wary of its excessively political nature and its adulation of communism. He certainly maintained relationships with the movement, realising this was in his interests – in March 1926 the new Galerie Surréaliste included him with Masson, Tanguy, Chirico, Ray, Rose Sélavy (Duchamp), Picabia, Picasso and Ernst – but he wanted to be free, and above all he wanted to work, for those groups were full of individuals who did nothing but talk and argue without doing a stroke. Miró frequented these groups, but within limits. And when he did, it merely reaffirmed his contempt for artists who spent their time theorising and his refusal to talk about his work and his feelings. His silences became legendary. But this does not mean that he did not open up when conversing with intelligent interlocutors or when asked reasonable questions that allowed him to comment on something that interested him.

Around the month of June, Viot suddenly vanished. It was said that he had gone to Papeete, in the New Hebrides, where he had become a justice of the peace. But no-one ever knew for certain what had become of him, except Gasch, who ran into him in Barcelona one day many years later, in the 1950's: Viot had by now become a well-known scriptwriter for the film director Marcel Carné. Miró was not affected

Joan Miró in Paris in 1927, with Arp, Mesens and Goemans.

by Viot's disappearance, although at that moment he was naturally worried because Viot had been his protector and he was afraid that fly-by-night act would jeopardise the gallery and its artists. Ernst warned him to take all the necessary precautions regarding the studio he had rented in Rue Tourlaque, since it was in Viot's name and the police, who had orders to arrest him, could seize everything it contained in order to cover his debts. But everything was settled by other means, and Loeb guaranteed the continuity of the Gallery Pierre and presented Miró with a contract which provided for the purchase of all of his work. Miró had always felt a weakness for Viot, and admired his courage and immense capacity for running risks, and in later life he insisted on this point, admitting to Gasch that Viot had been the only person able or willing to take a chance on him. Loeb was a different kettle of fish, and moreover he did not believe in Miró's work: "His painting makes you die laughing," he used to say. The recognition that Miró was now beginning to earn was a prime factor in stabilising their relationship.

That summer, Miró interrupted his period of concentration in Mont-roig to accompany his widowed mother on a short stay at a spa in Sant Hilari Sacalm, in the hills near Girona. Then he returned to Paris for the winter. There, Max Ernst, who had been so helpful, who had written to tell him that Éluard wanted to buy *Harlequinade* and *Motherhood* and to offer him Arp's studio for 5,000 francs a year, suddenly began to act differently one night after a dinner where everyone had been drinking. A violent argument broke out and everyone had their say except Miró, who remained entrenched in one of his famous silences. Ernst grabbed a rope, tied it to a beam and threatened to string Miró up if he insisted on not taking sides. But Miró remained firm, and silent. The fact of having become the centre of attention had sent him into a kind of ecstasy. This is how Man Ray, an eyewitness, described the scene in his memoirs, and I prefer to believe him rather than others who were not present and have no doubt given flight to fantasy. Penrose, for example, declared that Miró was subjected to an interrogation and that Ernst, as if crazy, tugged on the rope, but his hands slipped and Miró was able to save himself by grabbing hold of it. But there is more to the story, because a few days later Man Ray took a photograph of Miró, and insidiously placed a rope alongside his head to recall the macabre event.

All of this had taken place in the studio Miró had rented from Viot in Rue Tourlaque, in the Cité des Fousains of Toulouse-Lautrec, Derain and Bonnard, located in an alleyway adjoining a parish cemetery in Montmartre. This move had brought him physically closer to the Surrealists, and he now had as neighbours Éluard, his respected friend Arp, the no longer trustworthy Ernst, and Magritte, among others. He stayed there until he got married a couple of years later. I wonder whether Ernst's overt animosity was provoked by the secrecy in which Miró worked and which he demanded of his dealer, telling him time and again not to show anyone what he was painting. Miró was afraid of being copied: this fear had germinated during Picasso's time at the Bateau-Lavoir, when with just a glance at a colleague's work he was capable of solving whatever problem the other had, with the result that in the end, at the cry of "Watch out, the Spaniard!" they would all shut their studio doors when he approached. Miró, who was searching for a language and an entire pictorial universe, could not risk showing his cards, particularly at that moment when his progress was desperately slow.

Some nights he went to the Café Cyrano or the bar in the Place Blanche, where passionate arguments took place; he, typically, did not participate in them, but he felt it necessary to show his face. He always arrived immaculately dressed, with the elegance of a British businessman, wearing one of the smart hats his friend Prats used to give him and carrying a Mexican walking stick with polychrome low-relief. The Sabadell-based journalist Trabat, who interviewed Miró at that time, made this comment: "You see him for the first time and you think he must have escaped from a shop window of tailor's dummies." In a word, Miró detested those who dressed as 'bohemian' artists. Prats said of him, "He has always liked to dress very well. He is dressed by a tailor from Reus, Queralt by name, who serves him with exquisite loyalty. He has always admired me as a hatter. Incidentally, I remember an anecdote concerning his good taste. It happened at André Masson's wedding, in Paris. Miró and his wife arrived so impeccably dressed that the vicar was on the point of marrying them again, taking them to be the bride and groom!"

That elegance and sartorial refinement led to him being nicknamed the "Marquis of Mont-roig," which no doubt amused him and must have seemed a joke of fate, having converted him into the owner of the property of the true Marquis. Miró did not give up his physical exercise: every morning he did a long series of Swedish gymnastics, followed by a good workout with the punchball; in fact he was so obsessed with keeping fit that he sometimes expressed himself in similes related to boxing, a sport that was very fashionable in the Paris of the time and even attracted the art critics. Due to his success and his presence at ballet performances, he began to frequent certain smart circles, as Maurice Sachs commented: "We were delighted that Captain Edward Molyneaux's wife and Henri Bardac happened to be sitting next to Adrienne Monnier and Sylvia Beach, that the Maritains were with Yvonne George, Miró, Lise Deharme and Princess Violette Murat. With envious eyes we watched Princess Sixte de Bourbon-Palma, the Duchess of Doudeauville, the Duchess of Croy, the Countess of Luppi and Prince Achille Murat take their seats in a private box."

Yet in his innermost self Miró had not changed one iota. He insisted that "I prefer a bowl of farmhouse soup to the ridiculously rich dishes of rich people." And to his close friend Gasch he said he felt "remote, whether here or in Paris, from the intellectuals, who are so cretinised all over the world, and I'm not at all interested in being a 'man of the world,' and I loathe those receptions in large halls, and I have no interest whatsoever in hob-nobbing with princesses." To Trabal he confirmed that "I'm happier going around in a sweater and drinking from a *porró* among the peasants of Mont-roig than sitting among duchesses in Paris in a dinner jacket." It is no surprise that he should declare these feelings at that moment, just when he had begun to suffer in the flesh those individuals and those ambiences.

It is somewhat paradoxical that, at the insistence of Matisse and his friend the Cubist painter

Marcousis, he was tempted to enter into the secrets of an art as ancient and traditional as dry-point engraving. But the meeting was very fruitful, and Miró went on to produce admirable work in the workshops of several engravers, such as Hayter, whom he met again after the Second World War in New York. At the same time, however, he had begun to adopt his radical, critical attitude towards the traditional practice of painting. He maintained, with a certain vehemence and a distinctly provocative intention, that painting had remained in a state of decadence ever since the age of the cave artists. What he meant was that it was necessary to search for the pure sources of art and, at the same time, to 'assassinate' the corruption that painting had suffered in order to escape from excessive intellectualisation once and for all. To achieve this, he insisted on putting aside traditional techniques and, in particular, experimenting with new materials. And this idea remained fixed in his mind until his old age. (We must recall that he staged an exhibition of lithographs at the Maeght Gallery which, significantly, was his homage to the cave artists, for which I had the honour of writing the text.) Fundamentally, this was a very Dadaist attitude, and Miró himself recognised this, even specifying that it followed the line of Duchamp; and he added that his rejection of beautiful things led him to use more sordid materials. As we can see, he was a creative assassin, since he operated from inside and with the aim of offering renewing ideas, not of annihilating or devastating what already existed.

The first of May, 1928, was the date of the *vernissage* of the exhibition Miró's dealer Pierre Loeb had organised for him at the Galerie Georges

Bernheim le Jeune. It was a strategy designed to conquer the rest of Paris, since the Galerie Pierre was on the Rive Gauche, while the Bernheim gallery was in the Faubourg Saint-Honoré and enjoyed considerable prestige in the city. Miró sold all of the works he put on show here, and the critics praised him to the skies. It was significant that New York's embryonic Museum of Modern Art bought two of his paintings, while the Gallery of Living of New York University bought *Dog Barking at the Moon.* It was Miró's consecration. His work also entered the most important collections, such as those of Gaffé, the Viscountess of Noailles, Doucet, Kahn, Cuttoli, Gallatin, van Hecke, Schwachenberger and Janlet. It was said that Honneger had declared that Miró's work was present in all of the galleries of Moscow, but I suspect this was a baseless exaggeration.

At that time Miró was forging a close and long-lasting relationship with the illustrious philosopher Maritain, who had been attracted to his work. This demonstrated that although Miró was irritated by the intellectuals, writers and artists who constantly theorised about painting, they were not all the same, and Miró could distinguish between them. He also met and immediately became close friends with Alexander Calder, forming a relationship which was to have a profound reciprocal impact.

The day after the *vernissage* Miró set off on a two-week tour of Belgium and Holland. This is what he told me about it: "I went to visit the museums. And once I was there, I began to take an interest in the beauty of the landscape, because this was the season when the flowers were in full bloom. Vermeer and the seventeenth-century Dutch masters interested me

83

a great deal. I bought a lot of postcards of their most characteristic and famous paintings. On returning to Paris I decided to copy some of those works in my own way. And I did it the same way as with *The Farm*, with the model in front of me. So I painted *Dutch Interior I* with the postcard placed on the easel. I had no intention of mocking Sorgh and his *Lute Player*. What happened was that the result grew out of the tragi-comic mixture that dominates my character."

IN LOVE WITH TWO PILARS

Despite his way of concentrating on the passion of his work, which did not allow him to be distracted, during that journey he certainly had time to study other things, and he also had time to write a few post-cards to his future wife, Pilar. And on this point there has long been a confusion which is now easy to clear up. On 29 March 1927, Miró had commented in a letter to Ràfols that "my fiancée is very keen to meet you." And on 5 June 1928 he announced to him, "I would like to meet you before I get married – on the 21st of June, God willing!" But he did not marry Pilar until the autumn of 1929. What had happened? The answer is very simple: there were two Pilars! Of the first, Pilar Tey, I know nothing more than her name, but everything indicates that she had an intellectual, domineering character and that shortly before the planned wedding she had a bitter argument with Miró's mother which made her decide she did not want to go and live in the Miró family's apartment in Passatge del Crèdit. This critical confrontation led Miró to make that journey to Holland. But the most interesting thing is that from there he sent an endless series of postcards to the second Pilar, his future wife.

Pilar Juncosa i Iglesias, born in Palma de Mallorca on 18 July 1904, was the third daughter of a family of eight children formed by the furniture maker Lambert Juncosa and his wife Enriqueta Iglesias, both born in Barcelona and of Catalan origin. Enriqueta was a first cousin of Miró's grandmother, and she and Miró's mother were very close, having lived together during their childhood. It seems Miró had set his eyes on Pilar, and at the wedding in Palma of one of Pilar's sisters Miró hoped he would be seated at her side, but they told him she had a fiancé: this unexpected news upset Miró so much that he retorted that he would go and sit next to the priest. The relationship was nipped in the bud until Miró's trip to Belgium and Holland, when he suddenly began to send her all those postcards. He took advantage of the wedding of Pilar's brother Enric, in March 1929, to get himself invited. In July he confessed to her, "I like you very much," which, Pilar has admitted, made her body tingle all over; and he not only declared his love for her but even asked her to marry him on her next name day. The courtship could hardly have been briefer. He described the events in a letter to Gasch: "I'm getting married on 12 October, in Palma, to Pilar Juncosa, the sweetest and most beautiful girl in the world, and without a trace of intellectuality." This final comment is very interesting, and understandable in the light of Miró's experiences. It is clear, then, that Miró made a very conscious choice of the kind of wife he wanted. And yet I suspect that later on he was not so sure, because she did not understand the artist she had for a husband and did not conceal this from him when he was admired all around the world. In this sense, then, his solitude within the family was complete.

The wedding took place at the parish church of Sant Nicolau in Palma. On his new bride's menu, Miró wrote: "To my wife, that I may never leave her side again and love her infinitely more every minute of my life. Joan." They spent their honeymoon at the idyllic Hotel Illa d'Or, overlooking the calm, peaceful waters of the harbour of Pollença, in the north of the island. Pierre Loeb wrote them an expressive letter of congratulations. Pilar's father shipped to Marseilles all of the furniture for their new flat in Paris, at Rue François-Mouthon, 3. We now know all of these details thanks to the confidences Pilar decided to reveal after celebrating her 90th birthday.

In his old age, this is what Miró told Raillard about that transcendental step of getting married: "She liked me. She has great respect for me, but that's on the outside. I would have hated to have a wife who wanted to dictate to me. I prefer her like that. She's the ideal companion for me. Without her, I'd be an orphan lost in the world: outside of my work I've got no idea about anything nor about how to organise myself. She's my guardian angel."

This was, without doubt, a transcendental decision which was to have a profound influence on his life. Marriage was unknown territory: it was a matter that had never obsessed him nor even concerned him. But this does not mean that he had never thought about it. Jacques Dupin, his biographer and an expert on his work, has commented that he had problems of affection and communication, but what we do not know is if this was due to a failure to make himself accepted. Shyness, reticence or distance made it hard for him to establish relationships with women. He himself was struck by the odd manner in which he treated the female sex in his work, which sometimes displays a disturbing mixture of desire and violence. It is not known for certain that he had any love affairs before the two we have mentioned. Some unconfirmed rumours referred to a supposed relationship with a Paris showgirl, which left him with unpleasant memories and a certain amount of suffering. There is also talk of a Swedish woman. And some people have wondered whether the titles of important works like *Portrait of Madame K* might refer to lovers. The same has been said about *Portrait of Madame B*, and in this case there are more indications of a basis in reality: on the preparatory drawing Miró wrote *Mademoiselle*, and it is not unreasonable to surmise that the initial 'B' corresponds to the name of Bianca, a lover with whom Miró had exchanged correspondence that was kept by his dealer Pierre Loeb; when Miró married Pilar, Loeb wrote to her asking if she wanted him to destroy those letters. In any case, what I want to make clear is that after his experience with Pilar Tey, Miró decided that the best profile for a lifelong companion was that of Pilar Juncosa. She gave him the stability he was undoubtedly seeking, since what he was really most interested in was his work. As a result, their respective responsibilities were clearly established from the very first day, as he explained to me one day at his Mallorcan estate of So n'Abrines: "Pilar rules upstairs and I rule down here." He was referring to the house and his study, respectively. However, it has to be said that at the beginning she started to clean a studio that until then Miró had taken care of, even waxing the floor: she knew that she could only dust and mop, and must not touch anything. She must have done this quite well, because afterwards he told her, "it looks like an angel has passed through the study and has cleaned it divinely."

Until their marriage, Pilar had led a very quiet, simple, homely, provincial life, and Miró acknowledged that she had been very brave in accepting the challenge of suddenly moving to Paris without the slightest transition. She did not know how to cook, she did not speak French, after just one month she found herself pregnant, and, as everyone wanted to meet her, from the very first day a whole parade of friends invited them for lunch or dinner. She plucked up courage and forged ahead, with the help of her husband's French lessons and the recipes her sister-in-law sent her. And in no time at all she had not merely taken control of the situation but, for example, her *paellas* had rapidly become famous, as Picasso loved to report. They were getting along, if modestly. Miró had to paint at home, in one of the three bedrooms in the apartment, because he could not afford to rent a studio as well. The decoration of the apartment included the saddlebags of a Toledo mule, a black sculpture which was no doubt a wedding present from Loeb, and the horrific mouth of a shark Hemingway had caught off the coast of Florida and had sent with the photographs of the feat, one of which showed a human hand that had been found in its belly. There was not a single work by Miró himself in the house: "I can't bear looking at my work. I haven't hung any of my paintings at home, and I haven't allowed my wife to do so," he said shortly after the wedding.

Then the Wall Street Crash occurred, immediately shaking the foundations of the art world, including

Paris, and soon Loeb told Miró that he was no longer in a position to continue buying all of his production. As a result, Miró simply backtracked and concentrated on working in small formats, which in fact was not at all inconvenient because he was painting in a very small room in the apartment. Nothing discouraged him, neither the new adverse external circumstances nor the most outspoken criticisms of his art, since any attacks merely reaffirmed his self-esteem and certainty that he had come into this world – and Catalonia – to fulfil a providential mission which he sometimes expressed very ingenuously. Francesc Pujols had slyly proclaimed that "there will come a day when we Catalans, for the simple fact of being Catalans, will have everything paid for us all around the world," and Miró was more or less convinced of something similar. Nevertheless, talking to the journalist Trabat he said, "I remember with absolute hatred hearing the Orfeó Català sing that dismal song *L'emigrant* that goes 'Sweet Catalonia, homeland of my heart, far from you one dies of longing' I am convinced that in nationalism impact is always preferable to sentimentalism, and instead of singing funeral hymns our young men should be singing warrior chants."

These principles seem to me to be exemplary, but sometimes Miró based his position and certain aspects of his work on rather simplistic arguments which centred on a transcendentalist destiny. For this reason, as Llorens i Artigas has related, his Catalan friends in Paris conspired to make him believe that an aura had suddenly appeared around him ... and Miró, credulous as he was, put his hands to his head to feel it. In the 1960's, knowing the story of the joke, his close friend the photographer Català Roca made a rear-view portrait of him surrounded by the triptych *The Hope of the Condemned Man,* seating him in such a way that the light from a spotlamp half-concealed behind his head produced the effect of a halo. The painter Ynglada comments in his memoirs that these were not the only practical jokes, some of them excessive, that Miró accepted with his countryman's calm and forbearance.

He was also convinced that certain events were prophetic; he had no doubt about the force of destiny, and he fondly cultivated a belief in what he did not hesitate to call the God of Chance, in this case as the starting point of a painting or his own enriching experience during the production of it. He went so far as to state, "I believe in dark forces and in astrology. I am Taurus with Scorpio rising, and perhaps this is why there are circles and spheres in so many of my pictures, evoking the rule of the planets."

Miró made calculated visits to the Surrealists of Rue Fontaine, to witness their debates on topical matters or their games of cards, tarot or *cadavres exquis.* And no doubt some private collection still conserves certain extravagant figures created by the impromptu but highly intuitive collaboration of Miró (the head), Ernst (the body) and Tanguy (the legs). In both Rue Fontaine and Rue du Château, both lorded over by Breton, they played the so-called 'game of truth,' which consisted in a ruthless interrogation of the most intimate details of the sexuality of each member of the group, which led to a number of expulsions, since Breton did not tolerate the slightest trace of explicit homosexuality. In this respect, Dalí once commented to me that "the Surrealist group

Pilar Juncosa and Joan Miró walking across the mosaic of the Pla de l'Os, in the Rambla of Barcelona.

was a bunch of pederasts who were in love with Breton. They all idolised him and he enjoyed exercising his impeccable dictatorship over them. He was influenced by German Romanticism and did not admit homosexuality within the group, and that is what caused his break with Cocteau. Every time the group decided to play the 'game of truth,' many of them had no alternative but to lie." In 1929 Breton sent them all a letter which aimed to bind them to his ideological and even political commitment; Miró replied that he was against taking a common action. For this reason he did not want to sign the manifesto of 1930, but equally did not want to break with them because he thought this was not in his interests. On perceiving that Miró had marked out a certain distance, and knowing him to be the leading Surrealist of them all, Breton asked him to visit them more often, but Miró did not appear as often as the guru would have liked, because he considered him a kind of Pope surrounded by yes-men, and he excused himself with a not very convincing "I can't, I don't have time."

In reality, Miró frequented the group as if he were making a Sunday visit to the family, and never took part in the ideological debates. "He kept himself intáct," Masson said; and Dupin gave a brilliant definition in saying that he was a believer but not a practising believer. A couple of years later, in 1931, he reaffirmed his position in an interview with a journalist from Madrid: "I consider Surrealism to be a very interesting intellectual phenomenon, but I don't want to bind myself to it with a severe discipline. They form a battalion, a company, and everything they do is strictly disciplined. I want to be independent."

Although the Galerie Pierre was suffering from the crisis, which directly affected Miró's economic resources, this did not harm his relationship with Loeb himself. Quite to the contrary: when Loeb visited Mallorca, Pilar's family offered him their fullest hospitality, and Miró was delighted to paint two *make-mono* murals of 2.5 metres for Loeb's daughter Florence's room. In fact, Loeb's house, with a dining room decorated by Bonnard, was by now almost a museum.

The same austerity that characterised the Paris apartment had also been imposed on Miró's study in

Mont-roig, which Gasch described as follows in the early 1930's: "Smooth white walls, whose cleanness was not violated by pictures, something Miró detested. The only things pinned up here and there were a few cardboard coffee mats. The distribution of these circles followed a clearly determined rhythm (...) A striking boxing poster rounded off the whole. And on the table there was a collection of whistles." Gasch was accompanied on that visit by Prats, Gomis and Carl Einstein, and Miró gave them a premiere of his first objects and assemblies, which made Gasch remark to Einstein that he was sure Miró would soon be moving into sculpture. That summer was a little different from the others, firstly because of the anticipation of an expected event and secondly because of the changes it was bound to cause: the birth of Miró's daughter Dolors, his first and only child, on 17 July 1930 at the family home in Barcelona. As a result of this happy event, the stays in Barcelona and Mont-roig became longer, which led Miró to install a studio on the top floor of the house in Passatge del Crèdit, just under the roof. It was at least a solution, although it was so small that he could barely turn a large canvas around in it. In Mallorca they hired a full-time maid who proved to be a great help for Pilar.

The choreographer Leonid Massine, who in an exhibition of objects at the Galerie Pierre had admired the evocative originality of the whole and had been particularly fascinated by the happiness and infantilism that permeated those volumes installed with so much power and personality in the space, decided to go and talk to Miró. He was convinced that Miró's collaboration in designing the stage sets and backdrops for his next ballet, *Jeux d'Enfants*, could be decisive. And that was how it turned out. The première was held in Monte Carlo on 14 April 1932 to great success, with the audience shouting "Long live Miró!" In order to produce those innovative creations, Miró had settled in the city, where the company was based. The new experience stimulated him a great deal: it had nothing to do with his habitual setting, working alone in a studio and in two dimensions; now he was one more member of a creative team, and he had to verify whether his ideas could be realised and whether the dancers accepted them and could move freely. Moreover, he had to forget about being a painter and think more as a sculptor, as he had to install a series of objects in a space, the stage. The theatrical atmosphere, the fact of forming part of the company, the moments of tensions and relaxation, all of this thrilled him. And he was alone – or was he? As Dolors was still very small, Miró had made Pilar stay in Barcelona with her. And this is how, or so it seems, he began a relationship with the ballerina Tamara Toumanova, who was dancing the role of the Spinning Top and whose photograph was published in the catalogue of the exhibition of Miró's theatre work presented at the Miró Foundation. This was presumably the reason why Pilar told me years later that she never left Miró alone, and that this had been the only time. Later on, however, there was one more separation, almost as long, but brought about by a *force majeure*, the Second World War.

The exhibition at the Galerie Pierre opened on 12 December 1931 and closed on 8 January. Miró included in it his sculpture-object *Personage*, the result of putting together a wooden clothes stand, a huge peasant's umbrella, a tree branch and a three-foot-long wooden cylinder. But Loeb, realising the enormous phallic symbolism of the work, did not dare to show it. He stowed it away, and when Picasso visited the exhibition, Loeb said to him, "He wanted to pull our legs." Miró told me this himself, adding that not

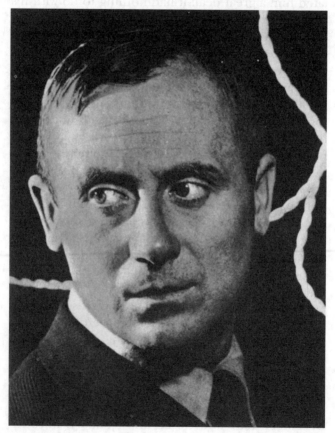

Joan Miró around 1930.

even his dealer was capable of understanding his avant-gardism. And he told Raillard, "It's true that there was a provocative intention on my part in the phallic exaggeration of the sculpture, but I also made it as a slightly ironic comment on the theme. After the exhibition, one day when Giacometti was with me in the Gallery, Pierre Loeb pointed at the sculpture and said sarcastically to him, 'That's to screw the chumps!' – and Alberto replied, quite rightly, 'in that case, it's too strong'." But the story did not finish here.

Henriette Gomès, Loeb's assistant at the Gallery at that time, has related what happened to that sculpture-object. Having stashed it away, Loeb decided to present it a few days later, that same month of December. The way Gomès tells it, she too failed to understand the work, both at that moment and when she wrote about it in the tribute catalogue to Pierre Loeb in 1979: "The day before the inauguration of the Salon des Surindépandants, Pierre asked me to take what Miró had sent us. I was met with laughter and sarcastic comments. Miró's work was a big Catalan peasant's umbrella placed on top of a roughly-trimmed piece of wood. It took me over an hour to convince the guards and managers of the Salon that it was not an umbrella but a 'work of art'."

The sad outcome was that work was finally dismantled, but I do not know when. In 1972, and at the initiative of the artist himself, who still had the wooden parts, it was reassembled and exhibited in the Miró Foundation. In this context, it is worth recalling what he wrote in his post-war diary (1941-45): "We must remember that for the primitive cultures, the non-decadent races, the sexual organ was a magical sign that human beings were proud of, far from the shame the decadent races feel today." Although the theme of sex was omnipresent throughout his work, Miró always refused to say anything about it. But with me he made an exception and agreed to answer all of the questions I wanted to ask him, in an interview which remains unpublished. In it, he insisted that what he was trying to portray was not influenced by the intention of resorting to eroticism, but simply that of representing sexual organs and copulation as part of a ritual and a ceremony with magical purposes, tightly bound to the mystery of life.

The birth of Dolors, the economic crisis that was affecting the Parisian art galleries, but above all a sudden decline in his mother's health, led the family to move to Barcelona. They lived above what had been Miró's parents' apartment, connected by an interior staircase. Despite the cramped conditions of the studio, Miró worked there until the outbreak of the Spanish Civil War in 1936. This new situation gave rise to a reunion with the city's timid avant-garde and a closer relationship with his nucleus of faithful friends like Prats, Gasch and Ràfols; but he also added new acquaintances who would also soon become close friends, like the architect Josep Lluís Sert and the cotton manufacturer and photographer Joaquim Gomis, not forgetting their wives, who formed close ties with Pilar. In this way an indestructible core was formed, the keystone of the resistance they were soon forced to display. In 1932, Prats, Sert and Gomis founded the dynamic group named ADLAN (Friends of New Art), whose mission was to promote avant-garde initiatives. Ràfols reported the visit made a few months earlier by a group of militants of the GATCPAC (the Group of Catalan Architects and Technicians for the Progress of Contemporary Architecture), like Germán Gómez of the GATEPAC (the same group's Spanish 'twin'), the critic Merlí and his protégés Estevan and Grau Sala; the poet J.V. Foix, the sculptor Àngel Ferrant and the critic Nubiola.

In this way, and as was natural and inevitable, Miró's relationships became closer, at least with those who were exasperated with the provincial-minded, backward-looking local art world and were opening their eyes to the international avant-garde, of which Miró was now one of the leading figures. The ADLAN was the group that inspired the influential magazine *D'Ací i d'Allà*, the *Vogue* of bourgeois Barcelona, directed by the refined writer Carles Soldevila, to dazzle its readers with an extraordinary issue – extraordinary in both senses, in surpassing its habitual high quality and in stepping outside its usual line to take a stance regarding avant-garde art. It is still startling today to observe how well-tuned the magazine's antennae were, because all of the creators selected then are now venerated in the Olympus of the art world. And it must be pointed out that the merit for this corresponds to the man who inspired the whole operation, once again Joan Prats, who as usual preferred to remain behind the scenes and avoid the spotlight. Miró's generous collaboration included painting not only the cover but also an intense circular *pochoir*. To cap it all, *Jeux d'Enfants* was staged at the Liceu from 13 to 28 May 1933, and it confirmed that Barcelona's Joan Miró was a creator of top-flight international stature who was respected not only in the art galleries. 'What a shame my father could not see this,' Miró must have thought.

On top of these successes, Miró had begun to make a name for himself on the other side of the Atlantic, having been exhibited by Pierre Matisse, the son of the artist Henri, at his gallery in New York. Miró managed to persuade him not to hold the *vernissage* until after the opening of *Jeux d'Enfants*, with the idea that this would give him free and influential publicity in the media, a fundamental factor in that society. I have always been surprised by the fine instinct Miró had for advertising, used with common sense and elegance, but he also had a knack for business, as we will soon have a chance to see. He had met Matisse in Paris in 1930, and it was not difficult for the two to reach an agreement, particularly in view of the economic difficulties Loeb was still suffering. Loeb was not at all happy when, in 1934, Miró signed a contract with Matisse making him his dealer and man of confidence in the United States and its zone of influence. Matisse later told his biographer, Russell, that the best thing that could have happened to his gallery was to achieve that signature, because its impact was decisive, and not only for his prestige. That first exhibition was a failure in sales terms, but the *vernissage* had been a considerable social event, being attended by the collectors Gallatin, Dreier and Scheyer, the composers Autheuil and Varèse, the artists Calder and Hélion and the writers Pound and Hemingway.

Around this time there occurred the break-up of a relationship which had initially been promising but recently had deteriorated further and further: that between Miró and Dalí. However, the cause was not a direct confrontation between the two. To explain it, it is worth taking a step back in time. Sometime in 1927, Loeb, generally well-informed, asked Miró to look at Dalí's work. Miró immediately took the Empordanese artist under his wing, and he wrote to Gasch and got him to organise a joint visit to Figueres that September. Dalí's work did not interest the dealer, but Dalí wrote to Lorca to tell him that it had impressed Miró. Back in Paris, Léonce Rosenberg was pressured by Miró into taking an interest in Dalí's paintings. Miró took Dalí to the gym to watch him practising boxing; he also invited him to visit his studio, where he marvelled at a bird hanging from a thread that Max Ernst had made from a simple piece of a chair; but most importantly, he introduced Dalí not only to André Breton at the Café Cyrano, but also to the Belgian dealer Goemans and the widow of the Spanish prime minister Eduardo Dato, now a patron of the arts. Miró attended the première of Dalí and Buñuel's film *L'Age d'Or*, where Dalí's father questioned him about the young artist: Miró defended him staunchly, asserting that he had a future as a painter. Dalí, for his part, did not attempt to conceal Miró's influence in his paintings, and in 1928 he published in the Sitges-based avant-garde magazine *L'Amic de les Arts* a eulogising article about him which appeared in a Belgian newspaper the following year.

It seems to me that Miró felt he had the responsibility to do for Dalí what Picasso had so generously done for him years earlier, because he sincerely valued Dalí's art. Pilar once said that when they were newly married they often invited Dalí and Gala to dinner; she commented that Dalí always wore loud ties and angora jerseys that left hairs all over the house, and that Joan was "fond of" Gala. But when the argument with Miró's great defender Gasch broke out, Dalí called him an "imbecile" in a series of furious letters and expected Miró to side with him and turn against the critic. But things did not go that way, and the rupture became inevitable. There were no scandals nor condemnations in the press: Miró simply maintained his distance as he had always done. Later, I suspect the situation worsened as Miró realised that Dalí had brazenly thrown in his lot with Franco's Nationalists in the Spanish Civil War. He always made it very plain that he detested the human side of Dalí.

Dalí and Gala were by no means the Mirós' only guests, for Pilar was becoming an increasingly good cook and she was very sociable, with the result that their dining room was often full of friends, including Picasso, who used to entertain Dolors with a game he made out of matchboxes which she still owns. At the end of dinner Picasso used to say, "At least when I come here I eat rice with prawns that don't taste of ammonia!" The secret of those *paellas*, Pilar has revealed, was none other than getting up early and buying the fish very fresh. They also used to receive Calder and his wife Louisa, who had recently settled in Paris and had a large packing case for a dining table. Calder used to like displaying his Keatonesque sense of humour by trying to stuff his shoe into his coffee cup.

Miró was careful to cultivate his close friends, and preferred to meet them in private rather than in fashionable restaurants or at the typical artists' parties. And he made lasting friendships, as with Kandinsky, who arrived in Paris in 1934 fleeing from the Nazis; the other Paris-based artists and critics shunned Kandinsky and scorned him as a schoolteacher whose painting was more like women's handicraft. His wife Nina recalled in her memoirs that he met Miró at a dinner at Loeb's house. Miró had been highly impressed by Kandinsky's exhibitions at the small galleries of Madame Zak and Madame Bucher. But while being a friend to his friends, Miró also felt it necessary to maintain certain balances, as is proved by the letter conserved by Matisse, which said: "There was a cake that Breton liked very much. It seemed prudent to me to stay on good terms with him, since the Surrealists have become 'official personalities' in Paris. Loeb was of the same opinion, and I gave him the cake. I think I did the right thing."

From the personal point of view, these were years of increasing intensity for Miró, as he was becoming known internationally and was having to travel more and more. He visited Brussels, Tenerife and Prague in 1935, and London in 1936. The only thing he was interested in, as he confirmed in the Proust Questionnaire that he answered for me in 1965, was devoting himself to his work, and he worked all the time, except when he was travelling, because he was aware of the favourable effect it had on him. The English artist and writer Roland Penrose met Miró during the latter's visit to London to attend the International Surrealist Exhibition organised by Penrose himself. He was with Man Ray, and they decided to go into a luxurious restaurant which had several dining rooms, each decorated in a different style. They chose the Egyptian room, and were startled to see Miró there, alone, half-hidden behind a large glass of ice cream with shapes and colours that looked like one of his paintings. This was Miró's ingenuous side, certainly; but Penrose goes on to say that Miró asked him to introduce him to some young artists, so he took him to Allen Jones' studio. Miró admired the picture Jones was painting – when he finished it he named it *Tribute to Joan Miró* – and in a sudden moment of enthusiasm Miró began to move chairs and other objects around the studio, piling them up to form a surprising monument which, when he left, had created an atmosphere that opened up new horizons for Jones' imagination.

Despite this festive air, however, Miró's work was beginning to reflect a tension, a violence, a horror, a desolation that threatened to be the end of everything. He constantly saw monstrous shapes, deformed limbs, scenes of extreme violence, infernally leering faces, skeletal figures that were a premonition of the Dantesque sights the world was to see later in the concentration camps: faces with gaping mouths, not in the manner of Munch, but savage, with the throats and teeth of sharks. Those demons he had begun to drive out with the big change he undertook in 1924 were nothing compared with the diabolical universe that appeared to him like an all-engulfing vomit. This is what he told me when I asked him about those experiences, and specifically about an electrifyingly representative painting from that period: "Unconsciously, I was living the characteristic atmosphere of unease you feel when something serious is about to happen. Like when it's about to rain: your head is heavy, your bones hurt, you sense a suffocating dampness in the air. It was an unease that was more physical than psychological. I had a premonition of catastrophe, but I didn't know what; it turned out to be the Spanish Civil War and the World War. I attempted to represent that tragedy that was torturing me inside. As you suggest, there is certainly a proximity between my works of that time and *Still Life with Old Shoe*. I hadn't realised! To achieve a powerfully dramatic atmosphere, drawing wasn't enough; I obtained the greatest aggressiveness through colour. Why did I give it that title? At that time I was obsessed with something Rembrandt once said: 'It is on the manure heap where I find rubies and emeralds'."

And since he was behaving in that fearful fashion before the canvas, he needed more than ever to conserve the stability and order that served as his counterbalance. And so, any one day of that period consisted in the following routine, maintained with clockwork precision: at six o'clock he got up, washed and had coffee and a few slices of bread for breakfast; at seven he went into the studio and worked non-stop until twelve, when he stopped to do an hour of energetic exercise, like boxing or running; at one o'clock he sat down for a frugal but well-prepared lunch, which he finished off with a coffee and three cigarettes, neither more nor less; then he practised his 'Mediterranean yoga,' a nap, but for just five minutes; at two he would receive a friend, deal with business matters or write letters; at three he returned to the studio, where he stayed until dinner time at eight o'clock; after dinner he would read for a while or listen to music. All told, an inflexible routine which he imposed on himself faultlessly and recognised as necessary to 'keep fit' as a painter. When he later moved to Mallorca to live, he liked swimming, as he had in Mont-roig, and when the weather was unfavourable for swimming he would go for long, brisk walks in the surrounding country-side. As he walked the beach from end to end, he was always on the lookout for some eye-catching object, which he would then install in a corner of his studio and wait to see if it would inspire a piece of sculpture. He continued with this open-air exercise until his old age, when his doctor finally advised him against it.

All of this was intended to achieve greater control over his own mind, and leading a healthy, ordered, balanced life assured him that he would never again fall into the pit of depression. And so it was. Once shut in the studio, his concentration was absolute and he dedicated himself totally to developing his work, and nothing and no-one could distract him. He confessed to Bernier, for example, that he even did some exercises that remind me of the ones Herrigel spoke of in his exquisite essay on the Japanese Zen archer; when he was painting the triptych *Blue*, he would prepare his mind by means of a slow, sustained rhythm of breathing. Knowing his character and his way of working, in which things evolved with agricultural slowness and in measured steps, instead of quickly and with improvised gestures, it was no surprise that he detested everything that would separate him or distract him from the only thing he was interested in: working.

Nonetheless, he was well aware that it was neces-sary to attend certain social and cultural events such as *vernissages*, or to give some interviews. He accepted these as a sacrifice, with an undisguisable expression of anguish as if he were going to the dentist's. It was

Miró's workshop reflected his tidy and colourful character.

for this reason that, when an American journalist asked him about these social events, the first word of his reply bore the stamp of Alfred Jarry: *"Merde!* I absolutely detest all openings and all parties! They're commercial, political, and everybody talks too much. They get on my tits!"

Another detail of his personality was his extreme and unconditional punctuality, not only in organising his private life, as we have seen, but also when travelling or receiving people. I know this from personal experience, because whenever I went to meet him at the Hotel Colón during his visits to Barcelona, I knew that he would step out of the lift exactly one minute before the appointed time. On the occasion of a long interview I conducted with him in 1969 to ask him about his adventures in Paris, we were to be accompanied by Francesc Vicens, who years later would create and direct the Miró Foundation. We sat down and chatted for five minutes, and on seeing that Vicens had not appeared at the agreed time, Miró said, with a slightly annoyed expression, "Let's start."

On 16 February 1936, a Picasso exhibition opened at the Sala Esteva in Barcelona. Picasso himself did not attend, but his close friends Éluard and Nush did. Texts were read out which had been specially written for the occasion by Sabartés, Juli González, Dalí and Miró. The event had been organised by the dynamic avant-garde artists of Sert's ADLAN group, who defended the Popular Front: it coincided with the Spanish general elections, and was designed to gather support for the left-wing coalition, which duly won the ballot. Éluard had given a speech the previous day at the Ateneu Enciclopèdic Popular, and was staying at the Nouvel Hotel Meublé in Carrer de Santa Anna. Miró was delighted to guide him around the city, and particularly to show him the works of the architectural genius Gaudí. In a letter to Matisse at the end of that year, Éluard wrote, "The erudite ones are not as dangerous as the *literati*: these are among the worst enemies of mankind. They must be treated as criminals and punished as such. Some of them are even capable of saying that Van Gogh was 'limited' and of treating Cézanne and Rousseau as poor lunatics. What an example of intellectual cretinism!" It is to be supposed that the targets of his invective were the Surrealists.

ANARCHIST DEATH THREAT

The revolt against Spain's Republican government in July 1936 caught Miró with his family in Mont-roig, on his habitual summer visit which he had only missed the year Dolors was born. Despite the gravity of the events confirmed by the news, which he must have followed on the radio and probably in the newspapers too, he stayed where he was without altering the rhythm of his work, experimenting with a new series of paintings on masonite, an original material he had never used before. The visual themes revealed an unrestrained violence, and Dupin did not hesitate to interpret them as a ritual of exorcism in the face of the disaster of the Civil War. A few weeks went by, and then a friend in the village told Miró, "You've got to leave right away, the FAI [an anarchist party] are out to kill you!" Miró was, if anything, more surprised than scared, for he had always declared himself to be a republican and anti-bourgeois. It did not take long to find out what had happened, as he told me in his old age: "My sister had married Jaume Galobart, a right-wing idiot. I went to the wedding and a local newspaper published the guest list, which naturally included me. If that hadn't happened I would have stayed: I would have tried to be useful." This was not a mere piece of bravado uttered once the danger had passed, as we will soon see.

So Miró, like Sagarra and other intellectuals threatened with death, was forced to escape, and it is untrue that, as has been said until now, he was by then already back in Paris finalising the works to be sent for display in the retrospective at the New York gallery which Matisse had been planning to open on 30 November. It was something more than a preparation, because Loeb, in view of the artist's growing prestige and the emergence of a rival dealer on the other side of the Atlantic, had an idea that must certainly have delighted Miró: to exhibit the works for just a few hours before setting sail for the United States. We know this from a detailed letter he wrote to Matisse on 16 November, in which he expressed his excitement over the success of that improvised *vernissage* and over an exhibition that was fated to be ephemeral: from 9.00 p.m. to midnight. The event attracted some five hundred people. The festive atmosphere became more lively, and undoubtedly more moving for Miró, when the gramophone began to play a record of *sardana* tunes. Miró remarked to Loeb that this created an atmosphere of open and sincere sympathy for Catalonia and Spain. Details like this touched Miró's heart, and *sardana* music was subsequently played at any event of this type, as I myself witnessed, for instance, at the great retrospective held at the Moulin de la Galette in Paris in 1974.

In her old age, Pilar provided some details about her brother-in-law Galobart, who was murdered by members of the FAI. "He was a very good man, very rich, he had property and he was very pious: he used to make his workers pass the rosary." Miró said, "My mother stayed in Mont-roig, where she lived in the company of the militia men, which seemed very original to her and even elegant." As soon as Miró had arrived safely in Paris, Pilar and Dolors went to Barcelona with the idea of travelling to Paris to join him, but they were unable to obtain passports. Miró attempted to obtain them in Paris, but to no avail, so Pilar went to the passport office in Passeig de Gràcia and spoke to the anarchist official in charge, named Corxet, and explained her case to him; she got the necessary papers, and she and Dolors were finally able to travel to Paris to rejoin Miró on 16 December 1936, moving into the Hôtel Récamier, in the Place Saint-Sulpice, where Miró had lived since his arrival. During their separation, Miró had taken a decision, against Loeb's opinion: "If they can't come to Paris, I'll go back to Spain, despite the risk; I would be a coward if I didn't," he wrote in his letter to Matisse, adding that he would be willing to return to Catalonia but had been warned off this idea by all of his friends.

In February 1937, the family left the hotel rooms, which were too small for Miró to work, and moved into an apartment in Rue Jules Chapin, but this also proved to be too small, so they found a new home at Boulevard August Blanqui, 39, in a building owned by the expatriate American architect Paul Nelson, who also lived there. Nelson was a fairly well-known professional by then, having designed several notable public buildings, like the Palais de la Découverte, planned in collaboration with Oscar Nitzchke. Hemingway's wife Hadley also lived in the building, and *The Field* hung in her apartment for some time before she sent it to New York. As this apartment, too, was a little cramped for working, Loeb, as attentive as ever, solved the problem by offering Miró a spacious room above the Galerie Pierre where he could work on his large paintings.

The gravity of the situation in his homeland, and the prospect of an impending tragedy with no positive outcome in sight, led Miró to turn back to a certain visual realism, as if seeking a solid point of support, connected with the earth, through representing themes more familiar to him. But he wanted to do this in his own way, for real, to the bitter end, with no halfway measures. For this reason, it seemed reasonable to him, and even a process of initiation, to return to the origins, by going back to the art school he had attended so unprofitably on first arriving in Paris: the Grande Chaumière. It was almost an act of humility, like the wise man's acknowledgement that "I only know that I know nothing." Almost certainly Miró thought of the lesson of the great Gaudí, who returned to the Sant Lluc art school in a vain attempt to improve his drawing skills, which had brought him such poor marks during his architecture studies. Miró likewise suffered the painful and disheartening experience of finding that he was incapable of learning to draw well, although the blow was less severe than the first time, in 1920. But this discovery did not undermine his interest; he continued to go to classes every day, and made almost a hundred life drawings of nude models.

Within his limited possibilities, Miró would send food parcels to his relatives in Barcelona and also to some of his friends. He and his family anxiously followed the course of the Civil War from a distance. He became aware of the need once again to use the canvas as a space of catharsis, and in February 1937, in the room above the Galerie Pierre, he began painting *Still Life with Old Shoe*. (It is notable that in the two languages he loved best, Catalan and French, the term 'still life' has a much more tragic tone: *natura morta, nature morte*.) Miró once told me, "I was very depressed and disconcerted. Now I'll tell you what was the starting point of *Still Life with Old Shoe*. I was living in Paris, at the Hôtel Récamier, in the Place Saint-Sulpice. Close by, in Rue des Grands Augustins, there was a *bistrot* called La Grenouille where I used to eat. One day, as I was walking out, I saw on the ground a broken bottle wrapped in a piece of paper. And I said to myself, 'I'm going to paint a still life of that.' No doubt I included the shoe thinking of Van Gogh's *Still Life with Boots*. I asked my wife to go and buy an apple. I stuck a fork into it; I wasn't thinking about a soldier plunging his bayonet into an enemy's body, it was simply an implement for eating it. I didn't intend the crust of bread to represent the image of hunger. The Civil War was nothing but bombings, deaths and executions, and I wanted to reflect that dramatic, tragic moment. I confess that I wasn't aware of painting my own *Guernica*. That comparison was made much later. What I do remember is being clearly aware that I was painting something tremendously serious. It goes without saying that colour is the element that contributes to giving it a penetrating force; it is the visual element that most directly catches the eye. The composition is realistic because that atmosphere of terror had me paralysed and I could barely paint anything. For that reason, I did exercises, copying from life at the Grande Chaumière school. It was precisely at that time, in a figurative, painstaking manner, that I did *Self-Portrait*." A letter he wrote to Matisse at the time informs us that the empty bottle was of gin and the crust was of rye bread; it also adds that the bottle, throws flames all over the surface of the canvas, like a house on fire. On another occasion, Miró stated that the apple represented Spain.

He was offered one stimulating commission, and accepted it without hesitating, even though it signified assuming an irrevocable public commitment: to paint a one-franc postage stamp to raise funds for the Republican cause in Spain. He used the same technique as for the magazine *D'Ací i d'Allà*, the *pochoir*, which was economical and withstood long print runs compared with the other traditional printing systems of the time. Margit Rowell, in her book dedicated to compiling texts and declarations by Miró, said it was Tériade, the art dealer and publisher of *Minotaure*, who commissioned the work, but she gives no further details, and I have found no more information about it. In the long interview I held with Miró in 1978, from which I have already reproduced a number of fragments, he told me, "If I remember correctly, it was Zervos who asked me to paint something to be reproduced on a stamp. This was shortly before the Republican Pavilion. The stamp cost one franc. A limited run was also made of this work, with an enlarged reproduction of the figure and this text handwritten and signed by me: 'In the present struggle I see on the Fascist side the archaic forces, and on the other side the people, whose immense creative resources will give Spain an impetus that will take the world's breath away.' I painted the figure of a Catalan peasant wearing a *barretina* because he's a character I know very well and he's a being who stems from the earth. He was more authentic than an intellectual. I wanted him to cause a great visual impact. That's

116

what's important: if I succeed, then it's easy to make him have an intellectual impact, too. Did I realise this meant adopting a particular stance? Of course I did. I abhorred everything I saw as stuck in the past, and I placed my hope in what seemed more human and authentic. I felt very scared after creating this work."

In the end, it was not issued as a stamp. I believe that this adoption of a position by such a noted artist, but one who until that point had been well known for shying away every time the Surrealists asked him to commit himself, was what led him immediately to be considered for painting a mural for the Spanish Republic's Pavilion at the 1938 Paris Universal Exposition. This commission was a stimulating challenge, but at the same time one in which he could break his neck: and by that I am not referring merely to the physical creation of the work, which he stood on a scaffold to paint. It was stimulating due to the venue, the chance to accompany his mentor Picasso, the opportunity to do something useful for the Republican cause, and the fact that this was an official commission from the Government. At the same time, and although Miró was keen to explore large formats, this was the first time he had taken on a work of this size, and moreover in the physical manner it entailed. But the result was exceptional, and it manifested Miró's artistic stature, being perhaps the first time he had done his talents full justice. He created the work in the second half of June 1937. It is 5.50 metres high and 3.65 metres wide, and is made up of six cellotex panels. I would say he had no doubt about choosing the theme for the picture: it again portrays a Catalan peasant with a *barretina*, this time clearly identified as a reaper – *El Segador* – by his sickle. This was another allusion to the people of Catalonia, and specifically to the reapers' revolt against the Spanish authorities in the 17th century, which gave the country its national anthem, *Els Segadors*, the words of which are even reproduced at the foot of the picture.

When I asked Miró to comment on his painting *Catalan Peasant by Moonlight*, from 1968, he made these clarifications which are directly related with the theme: "There's no reason to look for more meaning than what a peasant represents. I've painted a lot of them. There's nothing strange in it, because for me the image of a peasant is something tremendously powerful. He's a character I know very well, I've lived close to him all my life. I painted the moon because in my pictorial world it's a very important poetic element. It's no contradiction, as you think, that the peasant is working by the light of the moon: some crops are planted precisely at night and during a particular lunar period. Obviously the title also has a profound poetic sense, contrasting the hard, even brutal figure of the peasant with the poetic subtlety of the moonlight. This picture is a tribute not so much to Catalonia as to the peasant of my region, as a symbol of my country. Yes, it's a token of the loyalty I've always maintained towards my homeland."

It must be said that Miró faced up to the challenge with admirable confidence and decision, as is demonstrated by the fact that he set about it with practically no prior study. All he had was a small schematic sketch, which, needless to say, was a veritable explosion of colour. And he launched his attack as only he knew how, by means of a "direct, brutal execution" as he himself later said. And in two weeks it was finished. Once the Exposition was over, the mural was taken to

118

The artist with the author.

Valencia, the last foothold of the Republican government. No-one knows what happened to it after that;
Miró asked Sert to track it down, but the mystery was
never solved. The answer may lie in the fact that,
once dismantled, it must have looked like a stack of
meaningless boards, and in the chaos of the retreat
from Valencia, it is not absurd to imagine that someone may have made a shelter out of it in the harbour
or on the beach, while waiting to board a ship bound
for exile...

It is worth reflecting here on what the creation of

those two works signified. The episode that nearly cost Miró his life at the beginning of the Civil War did nothing to mitigate his republican and anti-fascist convictions, quite to the contrary – in sharp contrast with many other well-known figures.

By the end of 1937, Matisse had left Paris and Loeb was showing even greater attention to Miró, to the extent of telling him that for his 45th birthday, the following April, he wanted to give him a special present: a portrait of Pilar by Balthus, who was also represented by Loeb. Miró was so delighted at the suggestion that he insisted he and his daughter should replace his wife in the portrait! Pilar was annoyed at the change, but as it turned out the sitters did not enjoy the experience. Balthus painted with monk-like slowness, and the posing sessions, which took place after lunch, were long and almost exasperating, as Miró himself complained in a letter to Matisse. Dolors had to adopt a forced pose, sitting on the floor leaning against her father, and she tended to slide on the waxed parquet; in the end the artist drove a nail into the wood to act as a support. But this was not the only incident. The worst thing was that Balthus never let his subjects see the painting until it was completely finished, and this must have sparked the curiosity of the 7-year-old girl, who regularly walked up to look at the portrait until Balthus threatened her, "I'll tie you up in a sack and throw you away!" – an idea that was so frightening and at the same time conceivable to her that she yelled, "Balthus is a bad man and I don't want to go back there!"

I wonder if it was this painting that encouraged Miró to begin his own self-portrait. It was an exercise in realism that possibly helped him at that moment to return to drawing from life, assisted by the fact that the model met all the necessary conditions. He painted it, as artists usually do, in front of a mirror, but the one Miró used was the magnifying mirror he used every morning for his impeccable shave. It may have been the only mirror he had, in his precarious circumstances, but the fact is that it was very appropriate for a portrait in which the artist wanted to examine himself in minute detail, in an effort of introspection to discover what lay beneath the surface appearance. As it turned out, Miró left the portrait unfinished and did not resume it until 1960, completing it with fast, aggressive strokes.

Although there were no grounds for optimism, in a letter to Matisse in April 1938 Miró made the somewhat ingenuous comment that although the situation in Spain was agonic it was far from desperate, because he harboured the firm hope that some event would act in favour of the Republicans. He also said that he was painting better than ever, and that the blue tones he was using were in the manner of Fra Angelico. In a conversation I once had with Miró about the style of that extraordinary artist, he spoke of "the faith with which he applied himself," in the sense of an absolute, superior conviction; and suddenly he exclaimed with passion, "Yes, exactly – faith, *punyeta!*" using his favourite expression of emphasis.

His studio was his place of escape, but there was no evading his difficult circumstances. The war had made it impossible for him to save money, and he sometimes found himself unable to meet unforeseen expenses like dentist's bills; for a man who had always scrupulously attended to his responsibilities, these worries kept him awake at night. At this time, also, Miró's sentimental side began to show itself more, leading him to visit Rue Blomet, where he had had his first studio. The house at number 45 had by now been demolished, but one touching detail still remained: the lilac tree Desnos had praised in his poem. Years later, in Barcelona, he would follow a similar ritual; he told me that staying at the Hotel Colón allowed him to visit Carrer de la Portaferrissa and to gaze at the side entrance to number 18 that used to lead to Dalmau's gallery, where everything had started for him.

ESCAPE FROM THE NAZIS

In the summer of 1938, Miró was invited by his land-lord, the American architect Paul Nelson, to spend the summer at his house in the charming Normandy village of Varangeville-sur-Mer. Miró greatly enjoyed his stay there, and he amused himself by painting for Nelson a mural composed of four large panels in different formats. The two men's conversations became so personal that they even talked about the market price of Miró's works; and when Nelson heard what Miró received from Loeb and Matisse for a whole year's work, he told him that that was the amount they asked for just one of his drawings. In this way, Miró became aware of a reality that would influence the negotiations he was soon to have with his two dealers. For the moment, seeing that political events were making it difficult for Loeb to pay Miró the stipulated amounts, Matisse decided to help him out, a decision his competitor found annoying but had no option but to accept.

The terrible events happening around him, the uncertain future and the responsibility of supporting his family forced Miró to rethink a number of things. The fall of Barcelona to Franco's troops on 26 January 1939, despite being foreseen as inevitable, was a very hard blow. If Le Corbusier dedicated a large painting to the event, Miró felt still more deeply the need to seek catharsis through his work, and he immediately began a series of lithographs that were to become famous, the *Barcelona Series*. He had enjoyed the previous year's stay in Varangeville so much that he decided to repeat the experience this year, though this time renting a house called Clos des Sansonnets, set in a very poetic landscape and close to the house his friend Braque had inhabited for some years. He also met there the writer Raymond Queneau, who he was fond of despite being an intellectual and despite his complaints over Miró's reluctance to talk about his work. In addition to Paul Nelson, other people he met there were his close friend Calder, Loeb, Herbert Read and Duthuit.

But in September 1939 the Second World War broke out, with Miró still in Normandy. For a brief time nothing perceptible happened on French soil and the French began to call it a *drôle de guerre*, a joke of a war. But Miró decided to stay where he was, no doubt convinced by Braque's advice not to return to Paris with the argument that they were safe from bombardment because they had a Red Cross hospital nearby. The situation was very serious, almost tragic. Miró had lost Barcelona, and if he were now to lose Paris he would lose everything. The world, his own world, seemed to be sinking beneath his feet. But he still had the escape of painting, which allowed him to close himself inside a universe of his own making.

Now he reached the moment he had announced to Matisse while working on *Still Life with Old Shoe*, when he said he felt a desire to return to poetic paintings. Years later he told James J. Sweeney, "I felt a pro-

124

found desire to escape. I deliberately shut myself inside myself. Night and music and the stars began to have a more and more important role in suggesting my paintings. Music had always attracted me, and now, in that period, it began to play the role that poetry had played in the early 1920's." I wonder if it was impecuniosity that led him to choose an album of rather small dimensions; in any case, for a creator of his category this was not an important factor, and in fact it even contributed to the unprecedented intensity of the result.

He started the first work of a famous series, the *Constellations*, on 21 January 1940, in the face of the imminent devastating entry of Hitler's troops into France. He told me, "I was very pessimistic. It seemed to me that everything was lost. With the Nazi invasion of France and the Fascist victory in Spain, I was certain that I would never be allowed to paint again, that I'd only be able to go down to the beach and draw pictures in the sand or with the smoke of a cigarette. When I was painting the *Constellations*, I truly had the sensation of working in secrecy, but it was a release for me as I stopped thinking about the tragedy that surrounded me. I didn't suffer while I was working, although the small format made it hard for me. First I drew the picture in charcoal. It wasn't easy, so when I finished one I gave myself a prize: I went to have a coffee and an *ensaïmada*, a good prize, because I was penniless. Yes, as you say, the background was a starting point that suggested to me all the rest. And this is how it happened: in Paris I'd bought a pad of paper for cleaning my brushes, and the first time I did it I was amazed by the result. From that moment on, every time I finished one of the *Constellations*,

I cleaned the brushes on a fresh sheet, and that gave me the background for the next one. In Paris I met the cultural attaché of the Brazilian Embassy. It was he who took the 23 *Constellations* in the diplomatic bag to Pierre Matisse, my dealer in New York. The exhibition caused a tremendous impact. It aroused great interest and enthusiasm, since it was the first exhibition of European art since the start of the war. I gave the paintings poetic titles because I had chosen this line and because poetry was all I had left in the world." Miró also told me that in the *Constellations* he used the blue paint left over from darkening the windows of the house at the orders of the authorities as a measure against air raids.

Each picture took a month to complete. The German invasion and the bombings over Varangeville finally persuaded the Mirós to escape. On 20 May they were able to catch the last train from Dieppe to Paris, after an anxious wait of several days in the station of Rouen. Seeing the chaos, Miró said to Pilar, "You take care of Dolors and I'll take care of the *Constellations*." It is not true that his daughter had an arm in plaster: Pilar has denied this, saying that Dolors had simply hurt her ankle and had a slight limp. The family arrived in a Paris that was almost empty, and stayed there for a few days. Sebastià Gasch was by then living in exile in the city, and he saw Miró walk into the Castelucho establishment depressed and almost in a trance, moaning over and over again, "They've bombed Varangeville!" It did not occur to him to ask Miró what on earth he was doing in Paris. Matisse had suggested that Miró escape to Mexico, after making contacts and receiving the consent of the country's government. Sert and Masson, in contrast, proposed the USA. Pilar preferred to return to Catalonia. Without much thought about the matter, and despite the danger involved, they took the train to Perpignan. There they went to the Spanish Consulate, but the officials refused to give them the travel permits they needed. But the consul, in Miró's words, "didn't give a damn about Franco." I am sure this must have been the Basque diplomat Oyarzun, because when I was preparing my biography of the poet Sagarra, his widow told me they had also crossed the frontier around that time and she remembered Oyarzun's name and his kindness.

The Mirós caught a train for Barcelona, but on arriving in Figueres they were surprised by a police control. "I was scared," Miró confessed, "but my name wasn't on their list." They got off the train in Girona, where they were met by Miró's faithful friend Joan Prats, who dissuaded them from going on to Barcelona, where they were almost certain to be arrested. They went instead to Quintanes de Voltregà, where Pilar's father, Lambert Juncosa, was waiting for them at the estate that had belonged to Jaume Galobart, Miró's murdered brother-in-law. Juncosa, an opponent of Franco, assured them that their best bet was to hide out in Palma de Mallorca, at his house, because the country had suffered the Fascist regime for three years now and people were sick of Franco and the Falange. They took his advice. They had arrived without luggage, they had lost everything, but they were able to survive thanks to the generosity of Pilar's mother.

And so they moved into the Juncosas' apartment at Carrer Minyones 11. From that moment on, Miró told me with a malicious half-smile, "I became simply

Pilar's husband," in the double sense of going unnoticed and living with his in-laws. He improvised a studio in the porch, and was able to rent a house near Carrer del Mar from a character who was even more monosyllabic than Miró himself; he immediately christened it "Yes's House." Life in Palma went on quietly and discreetly, which was the most suitable state of affairs for the time being. Miró threw himself once again into the obsessive task of continuing the *Constellations* series; after an endless working day in the porch studio that was often freezing, he would give himself a prize: a cup of hot chocolate or a coffee at Can Joan s'Aigo. That custom was very typical of him, and he maintained it into his old age, as if striving to preserve that naïve, childlike trait of a schoolboy who has done his homework and deserves a reward. His jokes always tended to reflect this innocent sense of fun: once at the Maeght Gallery, after an *accrochage*, I heard him say, "This painter lad has promise, ha-haa!"

He liked to take long walks through the old town, to visit the cathedral, and afterwards to stand gazing, hypnotised, over the immensity of the Mediterranean, always the same and always different, which no-one ever described more perceptively than Valéry: *La mer, la mer toujours recommencée(* He also used to stroll around the Molinar fishermen's district, where he could rarely resist the temptation to pick up some discarded object that seduced him. One day he came home with a canary cage that had been flattened by a lorry wheel and hung it up in his studio; when Pilar saw it she cried out, "But people will take you for a rag-picker!" On one of his visits to the cathedral he was struck by an experience that "made my hair stand on end" – it was early afternoon, the immense Gothic nave was empty, and the organist was rehearsing pieces by Bach and Mozart. Miró was so enchanted that he went back to the cathedral almost every afternoon of that sweltering summer of 1941. He described the experience to Sweeney in this way: "I would sit in that Gothic interior, daydreaming and imagining shapes. The light poured into the darkness through the stained glass like an orange flame. The cathedral was always empty at that time of day. The organ music and the sunlight filtered by the windows would suggest forms to me. I hardly saw anyone during those months. But those periods of solitude were very enriching." And they inspired him to produce not only eleven drawings but also a few canvases, like *Woman Listening to Music* and *Dancer Listening to the Organ in a Cathedral*, both of which are erroneously dated 1945. This was a period when Miró was devoting more time than ever to reading his favourite authors, the poets: primarily Baudelaire, Rimbaud, Apollinaire, Mallarmé, Jarry, St John of the Cross, St Teresa of Ávila, J.V. Foix and Joan Salvat-Papasseit.

When Dolors finished school that summer, the family wasted no time in moving to Mont-roig, to Miró's own beloved and inspiring earth which he had not trodden for so long, and which he hoped would convey to him all of the energy he now needed more than ever. The international political situation, with the two focal points of Miró's world, Barcelona and Paris, now both under the heel of Fascism, had plunged him into an obsessive state of concern. But he refused to let himself sink into pessimism, taking refuge, as always, in the slow, tenacious, all-absorbing process of creating his art. He decided to have a studio built in Mont-roig.

What was most important to him now was to finish the *Constellations* series, which he had continued to work on in Palma. He created the last two in Mont-roig, finishing the last one, number 23, on 12 September in that summer of 1941. In his diary for that year he wrote, "You have to be prepared to work in the most absolute indifference and obscurantism / live to work as long as it is possible / and when you no longer have the means to continue working, close yourself even further inside / the palace of the spirit in the purest contemplation." It is moving to see to what extent he was determined to remain faithful to his principles and his work. I think he wrote this to reflect on and externalise his decisions, to be able to accomplish them to the letter, as if this were his own personal Decalogue. In those days he said that when night fell on the deserted beach of Mont-roig the footsteps of men and sheep were like constellations. He walked that beach every day, because his life in that almost mythical spot, since the end of the Spanish Civil War, followed that routine that he meant to maintain, even though the timetable had varied slightly. The tenant farmer's wife described it in this way: "It was as if he was going off to do a day's work, he always did the same. He would get up and start work; at midday he took a walk around the estate, went for a swim, ran along the beach to work up a sweat and stay trim, and in the afternoon he shut himself in the studio." It was after he had heard that the Nazis had destroyed his paint brushes in Nolde, and while walking along the sand beside the sea, that he made the remark I quoted earlier, that perhaps one day, not too far away, he would only be able to "draw pictures in the sand or with the smoke of a cigarette."

In 1942, two reasons led him to set up home in Barcelona: one was that he wanted to be closer to his mother, whose health was by now very delicate, and the other was that he was sure he would not suffer political problems there. When the last tenants had moved out, the family kept the apartment empty, ready to occupy it themselves one day. In the Mirós' house at Passeig del Crèdit 4, the first floor had been his parent's apartment all their life; the second was now for Miró, Pilar and Dolors; and the third became Miró's studio. Pilar took charge of the whole building. Dolors attended the Virtèlia school. From 1943 to 1945, Pilar's doctor brother, Lluís Juncosa, lived with them. These were times of solitude and anonymity for Miró, and particularly affecting as this was in his native city, although he was able to further strengthen his friendship with Prats and with the photographer Joaquim Gomis and his wife Odette. He also became close to the master flamenco dancer Escudero, who was living in a dingy boarding house in the Plaça Reial and who he had known and admired since the 1930's. Miró had always liked flamenco, having been introduced into it, and the world of the *café concert*, by Gasch when they were both young. Years later, in the late 1970's, after Franco's death and King Juan Carlos' assumption of the throne, Escudero was having serious trouble making ends meet, and he asked Miró, who by then knew the King personally, to ask him to grant him a pension. Shortly afterwards Escudero began to receive a cheque every month. He died without ever knowing that it was his friend

Joan Miró in the Passatge del Crèdit, where he was born.

Miró who was really his benefactor, and who even paid for his funeral.

On 18 November 1942, in contrast with the misery of life in Spain, Miró had the immense satisfaction of the opening of a retrospective exhibition at the New York Museum of Modern Art, presented by Sweeney, who also published a monograph on his work. (This was not the first to be published on Miró: in 1937 the Japanese poet Shuzo Takiguchi dedicated one to him in Tokyo which has never been translated.) Although Pierre Matisse had already put on a number of shows for Miró in New York, the importance of that exhibition was naturally destined to create a major impact, and not only in the USA: and indeed, it proved to be the beginning of Miró's worldwide consecration. He would have loved to be there, even though he hated openings, but the war prevented it. It is curious to note that he shared the halls of the MOMA with another retrospective dedicated to Dalí: two Catalan painters receiving this major tribute side by side – and they detested each other

On 27 May 1944, Miró's mother died after a long illness. Dolors Ferrà Oromí had been born 80 years earlier in Palma de Mallorca. Although in her last years she had passed on to her son everything she owned, he had never wanted to exercise his position as her heir nor even to ask her for money to buy an overcoat he needed. And even now, he waited until the war was over before making use of his inheritance. These are details that deserve to be told in order to outline the human profile of the man.

It was also in 1944 when Miró took a decision that revealed just how determined and far-sighted he was in seeking to make his way in life, even when faced with the darkest night. He went to meet his old friend 'Papitu' Llorens i Artigas, keen to try out a new style in the age-old technique of pottery. The idea had come to him on seeing an exhibition by Llorens in 1942, which confirmed Papitu's mastery of fire and enamel; and to show him what his idea was, he used the very same pieces Llorens had rejected as defective in 1941 while preparing the following year's show. This was the beginning of a collaboration forged

Joan Miró in 1944.

under the sign of friendship and in the spirit of the
avant-garde, and which would not only last until
Papitu's death but even continue after it in the person
of his son, Joanet. It must be said, however, that
Llorens agreed to make that initial experiment
more out of friendship than conviction, for he had
observed his friend's avant-garde treatment with some
scepticism and a certain apprehension. But his realistic outlook led him to reflect that perhaps he was mistaken, particularly when he witnessed the good re-

ception those pieces enjoyed. At this time Miró also succeeded in having printed by Miralles, and sponsored by Prats, the *Barcelona Series* of lithographs, that violent, harrowing denunciation centring on a sun the colour of mourning, used this time more out of ideological coherence than economic necessity.

NEW YORK, NEW YORK!

On 9 January 1945, an event took place which was historic for various reasons: the *vernissage* at Matisse's gallery of the complete *Constellations* series. They had come into Matisse's hands in a manner that was typical of the times, having left Barcelona thanks to the selfless generosity of a foreign diplomat: personally, I am convinced it was the Brazilian cultural attaché Miró had met in Paris. Naturally it would not have been just anybody, for Miró was extremely jealous and protective of his work. I would like to recall an interesting story in this respect. Adelita Cobo, a member of the ADLAN group who also did administrative work for it, owned one of Miró's works but found herself needing to sell it to pay for an operation. She asked Miró for his permission to do so, and he gave it. Once the picture had been sold and the medical bills paid, a certain amount was left over, which Cobo used to buy a gift of gratitude for Miró: I think it was a piece of jewellery for his wife. But Miró gave it back to her; I suspect he found it almost contemptible that one of his creations could be turned into money and therefore into something as detestable as an utterly bourgeois piece of jewellery. I also had the occasion to observe how the zeal he devoted to his work was reflected in the care he took over his dedications: for example, he used the term "Cordially" for purely functional purposes, but if the recipient was someone he sincerely appreciated he would write "Affectionately."

To return to the diplomat, I have every reason to believe, as I have said, that he was Brazilian, and that his name was João Cabral de Melo Neto. But he was more things besides. For one thing, he was a poet – he even became his country's national poet – and in particular he was a dedicated admirer of Miró, to the extent that in 1950, during his period as consul in Barcelona, he wrote and published personally a book on Miró with specially-produced illustrations, printed by his own hand on a Boston press. Well now, the *Constellations* were painted (in tempera, gouache, oil, egg white and pastel) on 23 album sheets measuring 46 by 38 centimetres: dimensions easy enough to carry in a briefcase or, particularly, a diplomatic bag. The truth was that when Matisse first saw them he was somewhat disappointed, because for some time Miró had been telling him in his letters about the progress of the works and he had come to believe they were much bigger than they really were. Nevertheless, the exhibition had an extraordinary impact, being received as the first great European artistic message since the outbreak of the World War. Moreover, the presentation text had been written by Breton, who underlined the seriousness of the moment by declaring, "No, the condition of art (the most adventurous and explorative) has never been as precarious as in Europe during the summer of 1940, when its days appeared to be numbered." And the fact that this series of works should see the light of day during a time of persecution, escaping from underneath the bombs, brought out to safety and freedom in secret because of being "degenerate," was like a positive testament to the commitment to life, the victory of liberty and poetic creation. In 1959 Matisse published a facsimile edition of the series, with a text by Breton accompanying each one of the *Constellations*, although by now there were only 22 of them, not 23, because the missing one had been bought years earlier by a collector for his mistress, and attempting to recover it would have caused him considerable discomfort. On the frontispiece of the copy he kept for himself, Miró wrote this dedication: "For Pilar, the radiant star of these *Constellations*. Joan."

Shortly after that great exhibition, still in 1945, Matisse's elder sister Marguerite, who had been a militant in the French Resistance, offered to take a large sum of cash (three thousand dollars) to Miró, even though this was strictly prohibited. The Matisses' biographer recorded that they could think of nothing better than to stuff the notes into toothpaste tubes, which was the very first place the Spanish police looked when they detained Marguerite. After she was released, thanks to the exercise of certain influences, Miró asked her in despair if she was mad, and scolded her for being so imprudent. Shortly afterwards he received a visit from Teeny Duchamp, also sent by Matisse. These gestures won the emotion and gratitude of a Miró who had always believed that human contacts were fundamental in any type of relationship. And they proved definitive when the time came to compare Loeb's behaviour with the Matisses'. Then Pierre Matisse offered to pay Miró everything Loeb owed him since 1942 and to sign a new contract. Matisse was honest, but too cautious and lacking in impetus; very different from Maeght, who will soon take the stage.

The war was now over; Miró, exultant, donated to the French Republic his large painting *The Bullfight*, which the French consul in Barcelona personally transported to Paris in his own car. Miró immediately tried to restore his relationship with Loeb, who he still trusted. Loeb was planning to reopen his gallery, and Picasso and Miró had offered him their support. But when it came to negotiating a new contract, new difficulties cropped up, and although the correspondence reveals Miró's negotiating skills, the fact is that there was no way of reaching an agreement that included Matisse. I suppose that the sense of jealousy that tortured Loeb betrayed him in this subtle and at the same time understandable triangular game which failed to produce a positive outcome.

Miró's recent resumption of contact with Papitu Llorens i Artigas proved extremely fruitful, materialising in a systematic collaboration in the potter's workshop in Carrer de Jules Verne. But they had not yet begun to create their most innovative and groundbreaking work, partly because Miró still did not have a dealer to encourage him.

After fulfilling an endless string of bureaucratic formalities, Miró finally obtained a passport to enable him and Pilar to travel to the USA. His entry visa, in contrast, proved very easy for Pierre Matisse to obtain. The Mirós arrived in New York in February 1947, and their first great surprise was when they were met at the airport by Alexander Calder, wearing a Catalan *barretina* on his head and driving a convertible full of wires and junk. Miró extended his stay until October thanks to receiving a commission that

From left to right: Rodríguez Arias, Josep Lluís Sert, Alexandre Cirici, Oriol Bohigas and Francesc Vicens.

was unusually important in its dimensions and public projection: a large mural (10 metres by 3) for the restaurant of the Terrace Plaza Hotel in Cincinnati. Miró was clearly capable of executing the project, in view of his success at the Republican Pavilion in Paris years before. In this case, instead of executing the picture *in situ*, he painted it in a large studio lent to him by the artist Holty, but before starting work on it he made several visits to the restaurant to immerse himself in its singular atmosphere. These were months of intense activity, no doubt stimulated by the contagious dynamism of the city. Miró took the opportunity to create a number of engravings in the studio of the same Hayter who had initiated him in the technique in Paris and who had been driven to the USA by the war and had established there his

141

prestigious Atelier 17. Other great pleasures were his reunions with Tanguy, Ozenfant, Duchamp, and in particular with his dear friend Sert. He and Pilar were living in an apartment lent to them, maid and all, by a certain film director. The composer Varèse lived in the apartment below, and Miró created a *pochoir* especially for him.

Miró described the skyscrapers of New York as "the Pyramids of the 20th century" and the pace of the city as "a punch to the heart." The intensity of American city life led him to seek relaxation in one of his great passions, sport: whenever he could, he went to watch night-time basketball matches, and he also enjoyed watching baseball, but what truly excited him was the raw emotion of ice hockey, and he tried not to miss a single match. One proof that Miró was entering social spheres other than that of museums and galleries was when a New York hotelier bought one of his large paintings and hung it in his home; meanwhile, his designs were beginning to be used to decorate glasses, ashtrays, drinks mats and other items. On returning to Barcelona, he wrote Matisse a letter unashamedly acknowledging that "I love your country, which has given me a new strength and impulse. But I'm happy to be home."

Meanwhile, in 1947, Aimé Maeght, an enterprising young dealer who had just entered the Paris art world, had successfully staged a large international exhibition of Surrealism at his gallery, curated by Duchamp and Breton. It was an indication that he was willing and able to do great things. And the following year, finally, Miró had the opportunity, from Barcelona, to return to Paris after an absence of eight years. He received a very warm welcome, particularly

142

from old friends like Raynal, Limbour and Queneau. And Tristan Tzara engineered for him an important individual exhibition at Maeght's gallery which led to the publication of the ambitious catalogue of the series *Derrière le Miroir*, with stimulating texts by Limbour, Éluard, Cassou, Joan Prats and others. Almost inevitably, Maeght became Miró's dealer; Miró admired his boldness and allowed him to prompt him into great artistic adventures that he had always dreamed of but had never had the opportunity to carry out, some due to a simple lack of space, leading him to write in 1938, "I dream of having a large workshop." This was why, from this moment on, he concentrated on new experiments in the fields of pottery, sculpture and engraving, considerably reducing his pictorial activity until 1955. (It has to be said that when Miró died, Maeght still owed him such a large fortune that the case ended up in the hands of lawyers.)

The fact that he was now back in Barcelona passed virtually unnoticed, which was partly a relief and partly an irritation for him. He was doubtlessly stimulated by the request he received from a group of young artists to visit him in his studio in Passeig del Crèdit. These were the members of the Dau al Set group, who wanted to restore links with the pre-war avant-garde. They all came away with a splendid impression of Miró, as was testified in writing years later by the likes of Antoni Tàpies, Joan Brossa and Arnau Puig. I suppose Miró was flattered by their gesture; and perhaps he was flattered even more by a proposal from the young poet and critic Rafael Santos Torroella, consisting of an exhibition which would be a kind of local tribute: to display at the Galeries

Laietanes all of the Miró works contained in Barcelona galleries. Miró accepted the idea gladly, but warned the organiser that he might be making a mistake, because the city was not in his favour. The project was carried out in 1949, and showed works owned by Sindreu, Gomis, Vidal de Llobatera, Prats, Ràfols, Sunyer and others. It was not a great success, but equally there were no irate reactions to it, barring one mocking letter received by mail, as Santos Torroella's wife, Maite, recalled.

In that same year another important change took place in Miró's life, namely a move to another house. For one thing, Miró's mother had died in 1944, her death notice being printed in *La Vanguardia* in the compulsory Spanish language. But also, Miró had developed a mania about a mysterious herbalist who had rented the ground floor of the house from him for his shop: he displayed next to nothing in the window and had only a dim light inside the shop, and Miró became convinced he was not to be trusted and even requested a court order for his eviction, but lost the case and was so infuriated that he decided to leave the building himself. The family moved to Carrer de Folgueroles. "Our flat is magnificent," he told Ràfols. He kept on his studio in Passeig del Crèdit until Sert designed and built the studio in Mallorca, and then he sold up the house where he was born.

In 1951, with his friend Ràfols, there occurred an event that illustrates Miró's character. Matisse, like Maeght, was visiting Barcelona to buy up at laughable prices all of the Miró works that were still in private hands. Ràfols asked Miró's permission to sell his portrait of him, and offered him a percentage commission. Miró refused, but said, "Allow me to suggest that you make a cash gift to Antonieta [a very helpful employee at the Dalmau gallery] – she's hard up and you'll be doing a charitable act."

Miró forged a close collaboration with Papitu Llorens, the fruit of their long-standing mutual confidence, which was to produce incomparable and original results on the international pottery scene. They had already created pieces that were admired by Matisse and Maeght, made in Papitu's workshop in Carrer de Jules Verne in Barcelona. But Llorens then moved to a very old, solitary farmhouse, El Recó, situated next to the Romanesque church of the small village of Gallifa, in the Vallès Oriental district. From the 1950's onwards, Miró would have no alternative but to travel out there – but the unexpected powerful, solitary beauty of the place bewitched and inspired him, and he admitted to me that he loved to go and stay there. I know the place very well, because when I was young my family used to spend the summers in the neighbouring village. Miró did not drive; and he used to travel there on the beat-up old Sagalés bus, and the journey was always like some kind of pleasant initiatic rite for him. Life at El Recó ('the nook') was idyllic, and moreover Llorens' wife Violette was an exceptional cook. And to cap it all, Papitu's irreverent sense of humour kept everyone laughing. Miró told me that he used to go to bed very early, and never without meditating conscientiously on what he was to do the next day: this helped him to concentrate his attention and to attack his work with dizzying vitality early the next morning.

In 1956, when he received the commission from UNESCO to create two murals, Miró did not hesitate to call up Papitu's son Joanet, of the tender age of fifteen. This was just what he wanted, a pair of hands and a mind that had not been constrained and burdened down with classical training, someone who could learn alongside him and so contribute to the new language he wanted to create. In search of inspiration, all three went to study the cave paintings of Altamira, in Cantabria, and Gaudí's wall beside the entrance to the Park Güell in Barcelona. Papitu was shocked to see that Miró was set on breaking all of the rules, but it immediately became clear that the result was destined to take everyone's breath away.

The sale of the family home in Barcelona, the money he had received from Matisse and Maeght, and the warm memory of his stays in Mallorca led Miró to decide to settle in the island in 1955. He was looking for more than a mere house, something like the farm of Mont-roig, somewhere more rural than urban, so as to have a garden that would give him space and refuge, peace and quiet. He was attracted to an 18th-century house in the outskirts of Palma called Son Boter, which had all of the characteristics he dreamed of – but it belonged to a descendant of the famous German eccentric, Baron von Munchausen, who refused to sell it. And so Miró bought the adjoining estate, So n'Abrines. The house was designed by his brother-in-law Enric Juncosa, and Miró wanted his studio to be designed by Sert, but despite the close friendship that united them, Miró did not dare to ask him for the favour, revealing once again his unusually delicate sense of prudence and elegance. In the end it was Pilar who made the request to Sert, who was naturally delighted to accept what was an honour for him. Just how seriously he took the commission is shown by the fact that he designed the system of filtering the powerful Mallorcan sunlight with his students at Harvard. Having found a successful solution, he then applied it in the buildings he designed for the Maeght Foundation in Saint-Paul-de-Vence and Miró's own Foundation in Barcelona. The construction of the house was overseen by Enric Juncosa.

Miró had always lamented not having a studio that measured up to the scale of his ambitions. As I have said, in 1938 he wrote, "I dream of having a large workshop." He explained later that this dream was motivated by a desire for space more than for light, because the more pictures he painted, the more inspiration he felt to continue working. By the end of 1956 it had become clear that the studio was a territory where he was lord and master, while Pilar ran 'the upstairs,' that is, the rest of the house. Miró's grandson once told me, with a sly grin, that whenever he had to call for his grandfather, he did so from the landing instead of going all the way downstairs. Pilar decorated the house in the classic bourgeois style, but she also included vases by Papitu in the window and paintings by Kandinsky, Léger or Braque on the walls, while a mobile by Calder hung from the ceiling. In the couple's bedroom there hung one of the *Constellations*: this and other Mirós now broke the custom of not displaying the artist's work in his own home. Ironically, it took Miró almost two years before he could paint a picture in his treasured "large workshop"; the empty space caused him a panic that paralysed him.

In 1958, with the money he gained from the Guggenheim Prize, Miró was finally able to buy Son Boter; a mysterious, intense space where he kept, among other things, a fossilised cat and the skeleton of a toad. On the walls of a house, rather like Goya in his house of La Quinta, he began to outline a series of sketches in charcoal. While taking possession of his new workshop, he began, in a mixture of patience and wonderment, to unpack all of the boxes he had stored at the Lefevre-Foinet warehouse in Paris before escaping from the city in May 1940, almost twenty years earlier. The impact of rediscovering that past was not entirely gratifying, and his inflexible critical spirit made him decide that some of the drawings and gouaches were not worth conserving. This, from an artist who considered his work to be above everything else; and perhaps it was for this very reason that he decided to sentence those pieces to the fire. He had always proclaimed himself to be honest and free, and he maintained this to the end, as he also proved when he fed a number of highly valuable canvases to the flames in the mid-1970's. He never worried about what others might think of him if he was sure of his decision. At the end of his life he did not mince his words about this: "I don't give a damn what people say or think about me. They all laughed at me in the Rue Blomet. I've never been a whore, like a lot of them have." And he never allowed himself to be swayed by the temptations of certain dealers, not even when Loeb himself asked him, "When are you going to paint something like *The Farm* again?"

From the very first day in the new studio in So n'Abrines, Miró applied the strictest order and strove to master that space by being the same as ever, even wearing the same apron he had once asked his father-in-law, the cabinetmaker, to give him, even though it had previously belonged to his own father.

Some works are born in plaster first.

Although he remained secluded in So n'Abrines, working ceaselessly and avoiding outside relationships as far as possible, Miró did not take long to confirm his early impressions of the Mallorcans, and when in his old age Raillard asked him about the people of the island, he did not bite his tongue: "They're idiots. They've lost the sense of Mallorcan civilisation. They don't speak Catalan. They've destroyed the landscape. That's why I don't have anything to do with anybody. My nephews and nieces speak Spanish; I never see them."

"I'VE NEVER BEEN A WHORE"

When I edited a special colour supplement of *La Vanguardia* in 1973 in honour of Miró's eightieth birthday, we spent a whole morning talking in his studio, then went upstairs to reward ourselves with an aperitif Pilar had prepared. I told her about the details of the supplement, and suddenly Miró said, "Listen, Pilar – let's see if these fools around here realise who I really am." But it was impossible, and a sculpture park that he and Sert had planned for Palma's seafront promenade never materialised, in the same way as his proposal to create a series of stained-glass windows for the cathedral was never accepted.

In Barcelona, on the other hand, Miró's position seemed to be changing. Among those responsible for this were the Gaspar family, who owned a gallery. One day in 1956, Joan Gaspar ran into Miró while he was waiting for the tram in El Putxet; he already knew Miró, having exhibited some of his works in collective shows, but when he suggested an individual exhibition, Miró replied, "You value me, and you do what you can for me, but people here don't appreciate my work." Nevertheless, in 1957 the Sala Gaspar presented two exhibitions of lithographs, in January and October; and in April 1959 it opened an important first individual exhibition of paintings. Miró always insisted on one thing: his first name must appear as 'Joan' in Catalan, not as 'Juan' in Spanish as was then almost universally compulsory under the dictatorship. There is no doubt that the honour of reconciling Miró with his home city corresponded to the Gaspars, thanks to the exhibitions they organised almost every year. And they knew how to set the stage for these events; from the very beginning they succeeded in bringing together the elite of Catalan society, which in those days represented a kind of nationalist militancy. I remember Joan Gasper introducing Miró one by one to all of the people cramming the gallery, telling him their names, surnames and a few details about them. I attended this ritual at the presentation in 1963 of *Album 19*, a series of lithographs. Gaspar introduced me as "A young journalist and a good Barcelonan!" Miró pierced me with his gaze, took my hand and said, "Ah yes, the one who wants people to confess about their private lives!" He was referring to the interviews for the 'Proust Questionnaire' I had been publishing for some time in the magazine *Destino*. I had asked him, through Papitu, if he would agree to answer those questions, but his answer was "Don't bother me!" The next day, I went to see him at the Sala Gaspar and asked him again, but he refused: I suspect that what offended him was that his answers would have to appear in Spanish. I had spent a whole month of my wages from the Ediciones Destino publishing house, where I also worked, to buy one of his lithographs, and I asked him if at least he would sign it for me. This he did in an expressive fashion, with the word *afectuosament*. Some years later I finally persuaded him to answer the questionnaire for a book to be published – in Catalan – by

Ediciones Proa, entitled *43 respostes catalanes al Qües-*
tionari Proust.

Every single summer, Miró continued to comply
with his self-imposed obligation of reconnecting with
Mont-roig and drawing from it the energy that so bene-
fited him. The farmer would pick the Mirós up from
the station in his cart to take them to the house, as it
was just a couple of miles away. Once they had settled
in, they relied on the local taxi driver, Francesc, to
take them around, which normally meant visiting
nearby spots like the chapel of Sant Ramon, the
ruined abbey of Scala Dei, the towns of Falset or Cornudella, or the clifftop village of Siurana, where Miró
loved to admire the spectacular views: he used to step
so close to the edge of the dizzying precipice that
Francesc never left his side for fear he might fall over.
Miró also used to visit Reus to see his lifelong tailor,
Queralt, and have some suits made. Since 1955 the
Mirós had had new tenant farmers, the Rovira family,
whose son, who was then around twelve, used to go
every day to collect the mail and *La Vanguardia*, and
once a week the magazine *Destino*.

Miró used to get up early and devote the mornings to painting, then go for his obligatory swim at
midday, followed by his Swedish gymnastics class,
which his close friend Joaquim Gomis once managed
to photograph in some detail. He completed his
exercise with long walks along the endless beach, often returning loaded down with some strangely-
shaped object that had taken his fancy and, as Prats
said, was already a 'Miró' as soon as it was in his
hands. Even when he seemed to be relaxing or amusing himself, he was in fact still immersed in creative
inspiration, but in a different way. He was always

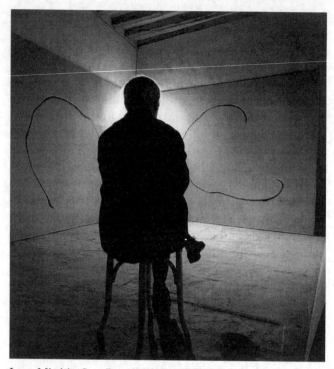

Joan Miró in Son Boter, Mallorca, 1973

working, like that day when he called me to his room at the Hotel Colón; it was just after midday, and when I arrived Miró showed me a sketch he had just made in his diary of the forms traced on the ceiling by the light filtering through the half-open shutters. He knew that this constant work was a vital necessity for him. One day Picasso confessed to him, with a touch of sadness mixed with resignation, "My friend, how lucky you are to be able to work in the place where your own truth lies; I can't."

In 1966, circumstances finally conspired to enable him to visit a civilisation that had always held a true aesthetic fascination for him: Japan. An important retrospective being held in Tokyo and Kyoto made his presence essential. In this way, he was finally able to meet in person the poet Takiguchi, who had written the first monograph to be published on Miró in all the world. He was so enchanted by that cultural discovery that in 1970, together with Llorens Artigas' family, he visited the country again, having completed the large mural he had created for the Expo in Osaka.

In 1968, Barcelona paid tribute to Miró by way of the large anthological exhibition dedicated to him in the solemn but thrilling setting of the old Hospital de la Santa Creu. The marriage between the Gothic stone slabs and Miró's brightly-coloured avant-garde shapes created a fascinating atmosphere. This was the reconciliation that finally allowed him to begin to be a 'prophet in his own land.' But neither Miró nor any of his associates attended the opening, on discovering at the last moment that it was to be headed by Franco's Minister of Information, Manuel Fraga. Another side of the coin was that there were still people in the city who laughed at his art and that the Museum of Modern Art only possessed one of his works, and an unimportant one at that, deposited by a private owner: a gouache that Pau Verrié had conserved since the times of the magazine *Ariel.* But it has to be said that the climate had changed appreciably and that the Gaspars' efforts had borne fruit. On April 20 of that year, Miró had the moving experience of seeing the official unveiling of a plaque in his honour on the façade of the house where he was born.

The opponents of official Francoist culture – young people, democrats, avant-garde artists and intellectuals – worked together to organise an event that would be the counterpoint to the pompous authorities' efforts to claim as their own this artist who had always represented precisely the contrary position. It took place at the Architecture School, which at that time still held high the banner of the counter-culture and the opposition. They staged the exhibition *Miró, otro* ("Miró, Another") to show his less 'friendly' side, that of rebellion, condemnation, the Dadaist, the anti-Francoist, and it could only be interpreted as an act of solidarity with the Catalan resistance movement. And for this reason the organisers made him a proposal that delighted him: to paint, in a purely improvised manner, the ground-floor windows of the School, with the vow to destroy them once the exhibition was over. It was a memorable event. Pilar was very annoyed because Miró had to get up at 6 a.m. But that was, after all, his style: if he accepted, it was to throw himself into the project headlong. When he finished, a debate ensued about whether it was really necessary to destroy the result. One of those who insisted that it was, Miró's biographer Jacques Dupin, said that the 'work' was not really a Miró, because he had only painted the black outlines, within which each of the curators of the exhibition added a different colour. He was right: the quality left a lot to be desired, and the creation was duly destroyed.

More and more factors were bringing Miró closer to Barcelona or causing him not just to visit it briefly but to stay as long as necessary each time, and always at the Hotel Colón. One reason was the magnificent creative relationship he had struck up with the Parellada family of foundry owners; they had been recommended to him by Clavé and he had hired their services since 1968, preferring them to foreign founders.

In 1971 I suggested to *La Vanguardia* a special supplement to commemorate Picasso's ninetieth birthday. They agreed and gave me *carte blanche*. The first thing I did was to ask Miró to paint the cover, and he accepted very enthusiastically. He produced a very large coloured gouache, which he dedicated to Picasso at the bottom. Once published, he asked me to keep the original at my house, saying that he would ask me for it at the appropriate moment: he wanted to present it to the master personally. But he never found the opportunity, so he then asked me to give it to Picasso myself, but directly into his own hands, with no intermediary whatsoever, not even his secretary Mariano Miguel. What Miró secretly wanted was for me to describe to him the reaction in his friend's huge eyes on seeing that picture, published in the same newspaper that had dedicated to him the first review of the very first exhibition of his life, the one held at Els Quatre Gats in 1900; and he wanted me to report to him Picasso's exact words and comments about the gift. It was a pity, but I, too, was unable to make the presentation. A few months later, Miró was finally able to do so himself. Picasso was delighted, and the painting, together with a copy of the newspaper, presided over the table that occupied the centre of a room containing some of his most treasured possessions; this was documented by the camera of David Douglas Duncan in the moving book of photographs he took the day after Picasso's death, at his wife Jacqueline's request. Miró visited Picasso from time to time, much less than he would have liked,

Support for the creation of the Catalan-language newspaper *AVUI* in 1976.

being accompanied in the final years by his grand-children. I do not know if Miró merited the same wry comment Picasso once made to Stravinsky, with an expression of puzzlement or reproach: "You mean to say you still live with the same woman?!"

On 12 December 1970, the Catalan anti-Francoist intellectuals locked themselves into the monastery of Montserrat. When Miró was invited to join them, he accepted straight away. He stayed there for a while and then left. Shortly afterwards, the Francoist press published some comments allegedly made by Pilar that seemed to question Miró's sense of commit-ment. The left-wing politician and writer Francesc Vicens, the future director of the Miró Foundation, rushed to Miró's home in Mallorca to persuade him to take a stand and make his true position clear. Miró asked him to telephone me personally at *La Van-*

Poster for the Venice Biennale exhibition (1976-1977).

guardia, congratulate me on a series of articles on him that the paper was publishing at the time, and ask me to publish his most strenuous denial. Naturally, I could not take a decision of such importance. I presented the matter to our editor, Horacio Sáenz Guerrero, who gave me a viable solution, to simply ignore the report just issued by Franco's news agency: in this way, it would not be necessary to deny a report that had not been published. That is what we did, and *El Correo Catalán* followed our lead after I made the suggestion to its director, Andreu Rosselló. At that moment, sadly, we could not hope to do any more.

Although Miró was now growing old, his vitality remained unaffected, and he was still able to maintain a surprising pace of work. His creative energy was stimulated by knowing that he was more in demand than ever, with commissions that demanded of him a physical fortitude that even he did not know he had. By then, he was alternating his studio work with journeys to faraway places like New York, London, Düsseldorf, Zürich, Milan or Rome. What continued to annoy him was having to attend openings, particularly if there were authorities present. In these circumstances his face was a poem, with a tight-lipped, absent expression. But he never said 'no' to anyone in Catalonia, as is demonstrated by the amount of posters he painted for innumerable civic initiatives and campaigns right across the spectrum of Catalanism.

Miró's daughter, Dolors, suffered a serious car accident, but she received such excellent care in the hospital of Tarragona that Miró decided to create a tapestry and dedicate it to the city. This inspired him to experiment further with textiles, with the decisive collaboration of Josep Royo, and led to the innova-

Woman and bird, a sculpture 22 metres in height, in the Plaça Joan Miró in Barcelona.

Monsters at the Liceu. *Mori el Merma.* A spectacle of surrealistic sarcasm.

The House with the Palm Tree (1918).

Portrait of a Girl (1919).

Self-Portrait (1919).

The Table (Still Life with Rabbit) (1920).

The Farm (1921-1922).

The Farmer's Wife (1922-1923).

Harlequinade (1924-1925).

The Music-Hall Usher (1925).

Hand Catching a Bird (1926).

Dog Howling at the Moon (1926).

Man and Woman in front of a Pile of Excrement (1936).

The Beautiful Bird Revealing the Unknown to a Pair of Lovers
(1941).

The Hope of the Condemned Man III (1974).

Catalan landscape (1923-1924).

tion that Cirici called *sobreteixims* ('overweavings') because it went far beyond classic tapestry work. This was one more testimony of Miró's constant curiosity and drive to explore new creative genres.

As I have just said, he detested inauguration ceremonies, cocktail sessions and speeches – he never said a single word before an audience – but from time to time he would make a special exception. One example of this was in Paris in 1974. He was very critical of what had until then been considered the world's art capital, believing that it was the city that had most prostrated itself at the feet of money and commercialism. He denounced a Paris that stank of money and knelt down before Chagall's bouquets of flowers – and this was rare in him, for if he hated or despised something he would never criticise it, merely relegate it to oblivion. But on this occasion he was thrilled that Páris had offered no less than the Grand Palais and the Musée d'Art Moderne to house the impressive anthological exhibition dedicated to him. The appropriately solemn opening ceremony was presided over by the Minister of Culture, Alain Peyrefitte. But what truly made Miró happy was the explosion of joy and freedom that took place that night at the Moulin de la Galette, with the new craze of 'streaking,' *sardanes* danced by Calder and Sweeney at the top of their form and played by the pre-eminent Cobla de la Bisbal, Maeght in the role of *chansonnier*, and a gesture of political commitment to culminate the night: a large Catalan flag painted by Tàpies and dedicated to Salvador Puig i Antich (falsely accused by the Franco regime of murdering a policeman, imprisoned and executed in Barcelona), which everyone present was invited to sign. I added my signature, even though the assistant editor of my newspaper, Manuel Ibáñez Escofet, tried to dissuade me by saying the police were sure to take note of everyone who signed what amounted to a political manifesto. That night, with *le tout Paris* gathered around him, I think Miró must have relived the heady days of Dada and that first nocturnal exhibition at the Galerie Pierre.

Miró's rebellious spirit, his political commitment and his artistic curiosity confirmed how youthful his mind and body remained. In 1979, with Royo, he burned a series of canvases to achieve a seductive 'toasted' quality, but also to "say 'shit' to all of those who say that my paintings cost a fortune," and also to evoke his childhood memories of bonfires on midsummer's night. And he was even more delighted when he realised the scandal this rebellious act had provoked. He told me, "For all of those who only see a rising value in money and for all of those who only think of stocks and shares and banknotes, take that! I scorch and burn what for them are just millions, to hell with them!" In contrast, with more modest people he was kind and attentive. A very revealing example of his personality is the following event. One day, a popular tribute was finally organised for him in Mont-roig. An eleven-year-old boy, Josep Miquel Martí Rom, came up to him with a photograph and asked if he would sign it, which he did without hesitation. The following day, he sent Pilar to ask the boy's mother if the signature was clear enough, because he had not been wearing his glasses and was none too sure; if necessary, he would gladly sign the photograph again.

His sense of political commitment led him to produce a huge triptych he had meditated on for two years and finished on the very day Puig i Antich was murdered on the 'vile garrotte' by the Franco regime. Miró dedicated the work to him, but the title could not be used until after the dictator's death.

He once invited me to visit his home in Palma to see the engraving workshop that the engraver Joan Barberà had installed for him so that he could explore yet another genre: one more demonstration of his youthful inquisitiveness and energy, now beyond the age of eighty, bearing out Sartre's words, "age is the loss of curiosity." On that occasion he told me, "When I'm working in the studio I sometimes need to take a piss, and instead of traipsing off to the other end of the building, I do it on a big sheet of paper. Without touching it, so as not to deform the wet surface, I immediately begin to let myself be guided by the hand holding the ink stirring rod." This approach was undoubtedly related to his burning of canvases, but also with the cave paintings of Altamira, which he admired unreservedly not so much for the power of the strokes but 'for the purity of the

The Miró Foundation.

Joan Miró in front of the Foundation.

painters' attitude: anti-intellectual, anti-academic, absolutely anti-everything."

When the artist was finally able to see the materialisation of his beloved Miró Foundation – so energetically encouraged by Joan Prats, who, sadly, did not live to see it completed – he was filled with an immense joy. And proof of his generosity and simplicity of manner was that he refused to let the building be a mausoleum for his work: instead, he wanted it to be "like a sketchbook, in which I will fill only the first page." It opened its doors on 10 June 1975, but Miró waited until well after the dictator's death to inaugurate it officially, on 18 June 1976. In this way he had accomplished what he had announced years before for his native city: the mural at the airport, the mosaic in the Rambla, and the Foundation. But he was never able to create the large sculpture in the Cervantes Park that was to welcome people entering

Barcelona by road; this was to have completed a trilogy, for the first two works were conceived as welcomes for those entering the city from the air and the sea, respectively.

Miró's collaboration in 1978 with the Dadaist adventure of *Mori el Merma* was another token of his generosity. Working in Palautordera, his inspiration took flight and he began to improvise and create far more work than was required. His rebellious nature was also revealed once again in his use of Jarry's grotesque character Ubu to caricature Franco. I attended the world première in Palma, but I saw Miró much more exultant later at the Liceu, because to succeed there was, once more, his symbolic victory over his father and the bourgeoisie and those who had mortified him as a young painter.

Joan Miró surrounded by the performers of *Mori el Merma*.

Also in 1978, Miró was very gratified by the large anthological exhibition staged in newly democratic Madrid – in other circumstances he would not have endorsed it – where the opening was exploited by arts students to stage a demonstration for their demands. Miró found this thrilling and gave them his full support.

By now he was suffering seriously from cataracts, above all because they were preventing him from working. The Clínica Barraquer did nothing to ease his affliction, refusing almost rudely to carry out the necessary operation; in total contrast, Dr. Ramon Castroviejo placed himself at Miró's entire disposal and even travelled to his home in Palma. The operation was a success and restored his *joie de vivre*, to the extent that he asked me to write an article giving the world the news: "I can see again!" But that happiness was not to last long, for soon afterwards he suffered a stroke, and on realising that he would never be the same again, that he could no longer even draw, the flame of life quickly died inside him.

The end came, with unwitting but appropriate irony, on the day most signally consecrated to Birth: the 25th of December, 1983. Miró had asked to be buried simply and directly in the ground, so that flowers would spring out of his belly. His will had remained inflexible to the end, but despite having left his last wishes in writing, the worst thing happened: the political authorities took possession of his body and organised a solemn ceremony, and the ecclesiastical authorities did likewise, staging an orthodox, puritan funeral starring Cardinal Jubany, as Paco Farreras criticised in such meticulous, indignant detail in his memoirs.

In contrast to the usual run of things, as Miró became more famous he earned respect and esteem from more and more people: from everyone. And what made him greater as a human being was that neither fame, nor money, nor glory, could corrupt him nor alter in the slightest what he had always wanted to be since his youngest days: an honest, simple, generous painter, faithful to himself and a citizen committed to liberty and to his country.

BIBLIOGRAPHY

Diaghilev. Richard Buckle. Weidenfeld & Nicholson. 1979.

Impressions d'un fotògraf. Memòries. F. Català-Roca. Edicions 62. 1995.

El descubrimiento de Miró y sus críticos. Victoria Combalía. Destino. 1990.

Picasso-Miró. Miradas cruzadas. Victoria Combalía. Electa. 1998.

L'aventure de Pierre Loeb. La Galerie Pierre 1924-1964. Various authors. Musée d'Art Moderne de la Ville de Paris. 1979.

Miró. Various authors. Los Cuadernos del Norte. 1983.

Joan Miró 1883-1993. Various authors. Fundació Joan Miró. 1993.

Estel fulgurant. Various authors. Fundació Pilar i Joan Miró a Mallorca. 1994.

Miró. Jacques Dupin. Flammarion. 1993.

Memòries. Elvira Farreras i Joan Gaspar. La Campana. 1997.

Gosar no mentir. Paco Farreras. Edicions 62. 1994.

L'expansió de l'art català al món. Sebastià Gasch. 1953.

Joan Miró. Sebastià Gasch. Alcides. 1963.

La vida excessiva de Salvador Dalí. Ian Gibson. Empúries. 1998.

Joaquim Gomis-Joan Miró. Fotografies 1941-1981. Daniel Giralt-Miracle. Gustavo Gili. 1994.

Nou converses amb Jordi Mercadé. Enric Jardí. Pòrtic. 1985.

Els moviments d'avantguarda a Barcelona. Enric Jardí. Edicions del Cotal. 1983.

Kandinsky y yo. Nina Kandinsky. Ediciones del Cotal. 1993.

Man Ray's Montparnasse. Herbert R. Lottman. Abrahams. 2001.

Joan Miró. Rosa Maria Malet. Edicions 62. 1992.

El "marquès de Mont-roig". A la recerca d'una ombra. Ressò mont-rogenc. 1998. Josep Miquel Martí Rom.

D'un roig encès. Josep Miquel Martí Rom. Vídeo. 1998.

Mont-roig: tornaveu mironià. Josep Miquel Martí Rom. 2002.

El Pabellón español en la Exposición Universal de París en 1937. Fernando Martín Martín. Universidad de Sevilla. 1983.

Josep Llorens Artigas. Escrits d'art. Ed. Ricard Mas. Universitat de Barcelona. 1993.

Joan Miró. Vida. Josep Meliá. Dopesa. 1973.

Selected writings and interviews. Joan Miró. Ed. Margit Rowell. G.K.Hall & Co. 1986.

Cartes a J. F. Ràfols (1917-1958). Joan Miró. Editorial Mediterrània. 1993.

Historia del surrealismo. Maurice Nadeau. Ariel. 1972.

Picasso i els seus amics catalans. Josep Palau i Fabre. Aedos. 1971.

Creación en el espacio. Roland Penrose. Polígrafa. 1972

Miró. Roland Penrose. Destino. 1991.

Los años difíciles de Miró, Llorens Artigas, Clavé, Fenosa, Dalí y Tàpies. Lluís Permanyer. Lumen. 1975.

Miró. Noranta anys. Lluís Permanyer. Edicions 62. 1984.

Ceci est la couleur de mes rêves. Georges Raillard. Seuil. 1977.

Selfportrait. Man Ray. Thames and Hudson. 1963

Memòries. Enric Cristòfor Ricart. Parsifal. 1995.

Joan Miró. Campo de estrellas. Margit Rowell. Reina Sofia. 1993.

Matisse. Father & Son. John Russell. Abrahams. 1999.

Au Temps du Boeuf sur le Toit. Maurice Sachs. Nouvelle Revue Critique. 1939.

Salvador Dalí corresponsal de J. V. Foix 1932-1936. Rafael Santos Torroella. Editorial Mediterrània. 1986.

Unas cartas de Miró a Dalmau. Rafael Santos Torroella. IVAM. 1993.

Records i opinions de Pere Ynglada. Carles Soldevila. Aedos. 1959.

Atmósfera Miró. James J. Sweeney. Polígrafa. 1959.

Picasso i els artistes catalans en el ballet. J. J. Tharrats. Edicions del Cotal. 1982.

Revolutionaires sans Révolution. André Thirion. Robert Laffont. 1972.

Una conversa amb Joan Miró. Francesc Trabal. Fundació La Mirada.

Josep Dalmau. L'aventura de l'art modern. Jaume Vidal i Oliveras. Fundació Caixa de Manresa. 1993.